of **PSYCHOLOGICAL ASSESSMENT** *Series*

Everything you need to know to administer, interpret, and score the major psychological tests.

I'd like to order the following
ESSENTIALS OF PSYCHOLOGICAL ASSESSMENT:

❏ WAIS®-III Assessment / 28295-2 / $34.95
❏ CAS Assessment / 29015-7 / $34.95
❏ Millon Inventories Assessment / 29798-4 / $34.95
❏ Forensic Psychological Assessment / 33186-4 / $34.95
❏ Bayley Scales of Infant Development-II Assessment / 32651-8 / $34.95
❏ Myers-Briggs Type Indicator® Assessment / 33239-9 / $34.95
❏ WISC-III® and WPPSI-R® Assessment / 34501-6 / $34.95
❏ Career Interest Assessment / 35365-5 / $34.95
❏ Rorschach® Assessment / 33146-5 / $34.95
❏ Cognitive Assessment with KAIT and Other Kaufman Measures 38317-1 / $34.95
❏ MMPI-2™ Assessment / 34533-4 / $34.95
❏ Nonverbal Assessment / 38318-X / $34.95
❏ Cross-Battery Assessment / 38264-7 / $34.95
❏ NEPSY® Assessment / 32690-9 / $34.95
❏ Individual Achievement Assessment / 32432-9 / $34.95
❏ TAT and Other Storytelling Techniques Assessment / 39469-6 / $34.95

Please send this order form with your payment (credit card or check) to:

JOHN WILEY & SONS, INC., Attn: J. Knott, 10th Floor
605 Third Avenue, New York, N.Y. 10158-0012

Name _____

Affiliation _____

Address _____

City/State/Zip _____

Phone _____ E-mail _____

❏ Would you like to be added to our e-mailing list?

Credit Card: ❏ MasterCard   ❏ Visa   ❏ American Express
(All orders subject to credit approval)

Card Number _____

Exp. Date _____ Signature _____

TO ORDER BY PHONE, CALL 1-800-225-5945
Refer to promo code #1-4081
To order online: www.wiley.com/essentials

Essentials of Behavioral Assessment

Essentials of Psychological Assessment Series
Series Editors, Alan S. Kaufman and Nadeen L. Kaufman

Essentials

of Behavioral Assessment

Michael C. Ramsay

Cecil R. Reynolds

R. W. Kamphaus

 John Wiley & Sons, Inc.

CONTENTS

SERIES PREFACE

I n the *Essentials of Psychological Assessment* series, we have attempted to provide the reader with books that will deliver key practical information in the most efficient and accessible style. The series features instruments in a variety of domains, such as cognition, personality, education, and neuropsychology. For the experienced clinician, books in the series offer a concise, yet thorough way to master utilization of the continuously evolving supply of new and revised instruments, as well as a convenient method for keeping up to date on the tried-and-true measures. The novice will find here a prioritized assembly of all the information and techniques that must be at one's fingertips to begin the complicated process of individual psychological diagnosis.

Wherever feasible, visual shortcuts to highlight key points are utilized alongside systematic, step-by-step guidelines. Chapters are focused and succinct. Topics are targeted for an easy understanding of the essentials of administration, scoring, interpretation, and clinical application. Theory and research are continually woven into the fabric of each book, but always to enhance clinical inference, never to sidetrack or overwhelm. We have long been advocates of "intelligent" testing—the notion that a profile of test scores is meaningless unless it is brought to life by the clinical observations and astute detective work of knowledgeable examiners. Test profiles must be used to make a difference in the child's or adult's life, or why bother to test? We want this series to help our readers become the best intelligent testers they can be.

This volume in Wiley's *Essentials* series provides the reader with descriptions and interpretive information on the three most widely used behavior assessment scales available: the Behavior Assessment System for Children (BASC; Reynolds & Kamphaus, 1998); the Child Behavior Checklist (CBCL; Achenbach, 1991a); and Conners' Rating Scales–Revised (CRS-R; Conners,

1997, 1999). Using these measures, a knowledgeable respondent provides impressionistic ratings of the frequency of specific behaviors, such as crying, shoving, and talking out of turn. Two of the scales, the BASC and the CBCL, also elicit self-reports of the frequency (presence or absence) of specific behaviors, thoughts, and feelings. The BASC provides two additional components: a direct observation form that provides for actual behavior counts, and a Structured Developmental History that assists the clinician in placing behavior into a larger context.

Each measure has its strengths and limitations. Each is an inventory used with children and adolescents as part of the diagnosis and intervention sequence in schools, clinics, hospitals, and private clinical offices. Each is suited for use throughout the United States and in many other countries.

Alan S. Kaufman, PhD, and Nadeen L. Kaufman, EdD, Series Editors
Yale University School of Medicine

Essentials of Behavioral Assessment

One

APPROACHES TO STANDARDIZED BEHAVIORAL ASSESSMENT

WHAT IS BEHAVIORAL ASSESSMENT?

Most of what psychologists and educators assess is behavior. How many answers did a student calculate correctly on a math quiz? How many seconds did a child require to copy designated symbols under a set of numbers? How often did a parent focus on fine details of an inkblot when interpreting its shape and color? Did an adolescent redraw lines when copying a figure? Did a child diagnosed with attentional difficulties correctly reproduce a design out of red and white blocks? The answers to all of these questions are really nothing more than samples of behavior, even when examined as part of a standardized assessment.

Conventions of psychology and measurement have led to the application of particular labels to various aspects of behavior assessed by psychological or educational means. Thus, practitioners and researchers commonly speak of achievement testing, intellectual assessment, personality testing, and behavioral assessment primarily in order to distinguish the various ways of gathering and using information in school and clinical settings. At one time, behavioral assessment dealt only with clearly observable, overt behavior. More recently, with the increased popularity of cognitive behaviorism, reports of covert behavior such as thoughts, feelings, and desires have come to be included as a central component of behavioral assessment (e.g., Kratochwill, Sheridan, Carlson, & Lasecki, 1999). In using self-reports of internal or otherwise unobservable phenomena, the behavioral assessment field does not seek determinants of character or draw deep-seated psychodynamic inferences. Instead, an examinee's responses are viewed directly for what they represent: samples of behavior and reports of the frequency or occurrence of specific behaviors.

In addition to the roles of thoughts, feelings, and other covert behavior, the

DON'T FORGET

Behavioral assessment places an emphasis on what the examinee *does*. Many other forms of assessment emphasize what the examinee *has*: attributes, traits, character, and the like.

DON'T FORGET

Feelings, thoughts, and other covert activities are behavior, even though you cannot observe them directly.

behavioral assessment field now recognizes the significance of chronic, long-standing characteristics such as anxiety and locus of control, both of which generalize beyond highly specific settings. In fact, many traditional scales used by psychologists have also become components of behavioral assessment, but the interpretation of the results requires fewer inferences. This development, like the recognition of covert behaviors, contrasts with early conceptualizations of the behavioral assessment paradigm (e.g., Evans & Nelson, 1977).

Behavioral assessment, then, is not a specific or necessarily unique set of tests or procedures, but rather a paradigm, a way of thinking about and using assessment data. Assessment yields hypotheses about people and their environments. Early approaches to assessment sought to derive hypotheses about the structures and causes of disorders. In contrast, the behavioral assessment paradigm stresses hypotheses about behavior itself; these hypotheses suggest person-environment interactions leading fairly directly to intervention.

By *person-environment interactions,* we mean ways in which examinees and their environments act together to produce behaviors or conditions that neither could produce alone. For example, suppose that a 10-year-old girl has reading difficulties. These difficulties do not arise solely from the girl herself, as though she lived in isolation. Likewise, her environment does not simply impose these difficulties upon her, as though she were merely a canvas to be painted. Instead, a combination of influences in the girl and her environment act together to produce her pattern of reading difficulties.

Behavioral assessment also relies upon multimethod and multimodal approaches to gathering information about the existence and frequency of behavior in multiple settings. A practitioner may collect information using direct observation, traditional psychometric assessment, dynamic assessment, and other *methods* or overall approaches to the assessment process (Hoy & Gregg, 1994). Conversely, an examinee may have the opportunity to demonstrate learning or skill in many ways. In science, for example, a student may investigate a problem using laboratory equipment, give oral explanations of this activity, record each procedure and conclusion in a notebook, construct a model from materials found in the classroom, and answer paper-and-pencil questions. The written, oral, and other *modalities* reflect primarily the student rather than the assessment (Kubiszin & Borich, 1996).

METHODS OF BEHAVIORAL ASSESSMENT

Kratochwill et al. (1999) describe various behavioral assessment procedures as lying on a continuum from direct to indirect assessment. They place such procedures as questionnaires and clinical interviews on the indirect end of the continuum. Direct procedures for behavioral assessment include self-monitoring, physiological recording, analogue assessment, and direct observation and counting of discrete behavioral events. In this chapter we describe each of these techniques, but the remaining chapters focus on direct observation, self-report measures, and ratings of behavior by others.

Interviewing

The clinical interview is probably the most ubiquitous form of assessment in which all mental health clinicians engage. Behaviorally oriented practitioners have long recognized the value of this procedure as an assessment method. The traditional clinical interview begins with an elicitation of the presenting problem, such as, "What brings you here?" "How can I help you?" or, directed to a parent, "Why did you want me to see your child?" After bringing out the presenting problem, the practitioner obtains a history of this problem, its context, and some developmental history. Compared with a clinical interview, a behavioral interview differs both conceptually and practically in its focus on problem solving and its search for the antecedents of a problem behavior. In addition, behavioral interviewing seeks to define the presenting problem in be-

DON'T FORGET
....
Behavioral interviews focus on problem-solving strategies and define presenting problems in terms of people's actions rather than their states, traits, or psychodynamic conflicts.

DON'T FORGET
....

Steps in Behavioral Interviewing

- Identify the problem and specify target behaviors.
- Identify and analyze relevant environmental factors.
- Develop a plan for intervention.
- Implement this plan.
- Evaluate the outcomes of treatment.
- Modify treatment as needed and reevaluate outcomes.

havioral terms, referring to specific actions—overt or covert—as opposed to states or traits.

A problem-solving approach to the interview process begins with problem identification and definition, including designation of target behaviors. Next, the practitioner seeks to determine what environmental factors are related to the occurrence of the identified problem. From this information comes a plan for intervention, implementation of the intervention, subsequent evaluation of outcomes, and modification of the treatment plan.

The flexibility of behavioral interviewing yields many advantages over more formal or standardized assessments. Practitioners can use the behavioral interview to obtain general information about examinees and their environments, to evaluate broad areas of functioning, and to gather details about specific areas of functioning or problems unique to the client. An examinee's responses often suggest follow-up questions, but these questions follow a trail of current environmental events or conditions. Behavioral interviewing seeks only the factors that sustain a behavior, not the early causes that first gave rise to it.

In contrast with more traditional, psychodynamic approaches, the behavioral interview seeks to minimize the amount of inference used to obtain data and looks primarily for current circumstances that trigger a behavior. This search, which varies from client to client, is the principal strength of behavioral interviewing. Nevertheless, rapport with the child and with people who are influential in the child's life remains important in a behavioral interview despite its contrasts with psychodynamic approaches. The interview gives practitioners an opportunity to interact at a more personal level and to achieve an alliance and rapport less well-afforded by formal, standardized testing. The behavioral interview is also eminently practical.

These strengths lead to some inevitable weaknesses. The lack of a standard protocol for the interview considerably limits the reliability and validity that can be obtained (see Chapter 2 for definitions of both terms). These problems were recognized early in the development of behavioral assessment as a conceptual approach to client presentation (e.g., see Cone, 1977, for a surprisingly current view of the issues). The extent to which two interviewers, each trained in behavioral techniques, ask similar follow-up questions, arrive at a common designation of the circumstantial trigger, and identify the same target behaviors is relatively low.

The consistency of behavior over time is a concern in developing interventions and interview techniques without quantifiable outcomes do not assess it accurately. This limitation has retarded research on behavioral interviewing. Despite more than 30 years of application, studies remain quite sparse. (See reviews in Kratochwill et al., 1999, and Ollendick & Greene, 1998.)

Self-Report Inventories

Another procedure for behavioral assessment relies on an individual's responses to a set of standardized questions and has an objective scoring system and a normative reference group. This self-report of cognitions, attitudes, feelings, and behavior—concurrent with the collection of interview data, ratings by others, and direct observation of behavior—introduces into the evaluation an additional component that is objective and typically practical as well. For the most part, information about internal experiences is accessible only through clients themselves. Thus, a *self-report inventory* is particularly important in diagnosing anxiety disorders and other conditions with a strong internal component.

Early in the development of behavioral assessment, practitioners avoided such measures, asserting that they were antithetical to the concept of behavioral assessments because only observable behaviors were regarded as acceptable data (Ollendick & Greene, 1998). Now, self-report measures have attained widespread use in behavioral assessment (Groth-Marnat, 1990; Kratochwill et al., 1999; Ollendick & Greene, 1998). This change has occurred for two primary reasons. Test developers have constructed a wide range of self-report inventories specifically for use in behavioral assessment. In addition, reports of feelings, thoughts, and other covert activities have gained recognition as behavior and indeed have become central to cognitive-behavioral approaches to assessment and intervention. Child self-report inventories have emerged in response to a recognition that children's perceptions of their environment, and of their behavior and its consequences, are important in their own right and in behavior change. Kratochwill et al. (1999) argue that, in behavioral assessment, self-report scales are most useful for gathering data on a child's cognitions and subjective experiences, information that is often unobtainable through any other means.

Self-report scales can be highly specific and tied to a narrow set of concepts (e.g., the Revised Children's Manifest Anxiety Scale or RCMAS; Reynolds & Richmond, 1985) or they can be of the omnibus variety, assessing a variety of constructs. The Behavior Assessment System for Children (BASC) and the Child Behavior Checklist (CBCL), two of the three instruments that are the focus of Chapters 2–6, combine their specific subscales into omnibus self-report scales. On the BASC, the omnibus scale is the Self-Report of Personality (SRP). In the CBCL system, it is the Youth Self-Report (YSR). Each scale taps multiple dimensions of a child's feelings and cognitions, thus performing the functions for which self-report scales are best suited.

Behavior Rating Scales

Behavior rating scales are typically omnibus, *broad band* scales: They provide for the assessment of a wide range of behaviors in children and youth. Some *narrow band* scales, such as the Attention Deficit Disorders Evaluation Scales (AD-DES), assess characteristics associated with Attention-Deficit/Hyperactivity Disorder (ADHD). Such instruments are not recommended, however, because they tend to overlook the many other disorders that sometimes have similar characteristics. These instruments lack specificity and are poor at differential diagnosis. The more broad-based scales associated with the BASC, the CBCL system, and the Conners' Rating Scales–Revised (CRS-R) are consistently superior to other scales and are by far the most widely used. Kratochwill et al. (1999) and Ollendick and Greene (1998) together describe 10 advantages to the use of broad-based behavior rating scales, noting that these measures

1. Provide an overall description of the child's behavior.
2. Elicit information on problems that may be overlooked in a behavioral interview and during direct observation.

3. Provide results that are easily quantified.
4. Allow derivation or specification of clusters of behavior that commonly co-occur for a particular child.
5. Assist in the empirical derivation of behavioral clusters common among groups of referred children.
6. Provide a reliable basis for comparing pre- and post-treatment behavior and evaluating outcomes.
7. Are a convenient means of obtaining data on the social validity of outcomes.
8. Typically assess broad dimensions such as school functioning, as well as narrow dimensions such as anxiety.
9. Are a cost-effective, convenient, and minimally intrusive means of collecting objective data.
10. Are useful in matching a child with a specific treatment.

To this list we add that behavior rating scales

11. Assist in making differential diagnoses among disorders, not just in detecting the presence of abnormal frequencies of behavior.
12. Permit normative, developmentally sensitive comparisons through empirical methods rather than through clinical judgment or other subjective procedures.
13. Can be evaluated empirically as diagnostic tests using familiar psychometric concepts such as reliability and validity.
14. Provide a clearly systematic method that can be used easily in the same way by numerous clinicians and in numerous settings.
15. May allow a prioritization of target behaviors, as with the BASC.

Despite these strengths and advantages, rating scales do present some potential problems and should not be used in isolation. Behavior ratings are impressionistic, holistic ratings provided by a respondent (typically a parent or teacher) who may be biased. The ratings received are thus summary judgments, albeit systematic and standardized, made by someone knowledgeable about the child, and appropriate for a comparison to a common referent, the ratings of the norming sample. In addition, children behave differently under different circumstances and under the direction of different individuals, even if their settings are similar. Practitioners should obtain ratings from multiple respondents when possible in order to assess the specificity and generalizability of the behavioral patterns detected.

Kratochwill et al. (1999) reprove behavior rating scales, regarding them as designed to detect the presence of negative behaviors (i.e., behavioral excesses and deficits) but not positive behaviors or assets of the child. The BASC, however, devotes substantial numbers of items and scales to such behavioral strengths or assets because the identification of both positive and negative behavior is central to BASC philosophy.

Direct Observation and Recording

Direct observation and recording, typically through a counting procedure, is another widely used procedure among behaviorally oriented practitioners. Some (e.g., Ollendick & Greene, 1998) hail direct observation of a child's behavior in the natural environment as the hallmark of child behavioral assessment. This form of observation is also a unique contribution to assessment from the behavioral school of psychology. Direct observation as an assessment method has four determining features: Observation occurs in a natural setting; recording or counting of behaviors is done at the time the behavior occurs, not retrospectively as with the rating scales noted above; impartial observers code or record the behavior; and the coded behaviors are described clearly, involving little or no inference for accurate recording of the behavior. The features of direct observation are listed in Rapid Reference 1.1.

Direct observation can occur with or without a standard behavior checklist or classification scheme but is easier to accomplish using a standardized coding system, such as the BASC Student Observation Scale (SOS). A standard format enhances training, objectivity, and accuracy, but reduces flexibility. To

Rapid Reference 1.1

Key Characteristics of Direct Observation and Recording of Behavior

- Behavior is observed in a natural setting.
- Behavior is recorded or coded as it occurs.
- Impartial, objective observers record behavior.
- Behavior is described in clear, crisp terms, requiring little or no inference by the observer.

promote objectivity, the observer should be blind to the presence of any intervention plans that are in place. Nevertheless, standardized codes for behavior such as those contained in the BASC SOS are the recommended practice (e.g., Kratochwill et al., 1999).

Observers should be as unobtrusive as possible or they may disrupt the natural setting and alter naturally occurring behavior patterns. Observation and coding of behavior in multiple settings (e.g., in two or more classrooms and with different teachers) also are preferred because this method assists in evaluating the generalizability versus the specificity of the behaviors seen. Direct observation of behavior is the least inferential of psychological assessment procedures, but issues of reliability are a major concern—one that is allayed in part by multiple ratings in several settings.

Self-Monitoring

Self-monitoring is a form of direct observation in which children monitor or observe their own behavior and then record it. An enormous literature in this area shows that children are capable of being trained to observe and record their behavior accurately, if motivated to do so. As with other methods of direct observation, it is very important to define the relevant behaviors clearly and with much specificity. A small number of behaviors should be specified as well, or the child may become overwhelmed or attend only to a subset of the behaviors given to monitor. Self-monitoring can be an effective means of collecting data on a few important behaviors' frequency and settings. Self-monitoring is obviously a form of self-report but is distinguished from the self-report scales (discussed previously) by the contemporaneous nature of the recording. In self-monitoring, the child codes or records the behavior as it occurs, whereas self-report scales are retrospective accounts of more numerous and varied behaviors, which are typically less specified than behaviors subjected to self-monitoring. Few standardized protocols for self-monitoring exist, and none of the systems addressed in this volume have self-monitoring scales.

Analogue Observation

Analogue observation is a method of direct observation, but it occurs in a contrived, carefully structured setting, designed specifically for the assessment. By contrast, direct observation occurs in a naturalistic setting. In analogue assessment or observation, after the setting has been structured, direct observation of behavior follows, using many of the principles of observation previously described.

Psychophysiological Assessment

Psychophysiological assessment is an important form of behavioral assessment that entails a direct recording of physiologically observed changes in the body, such as increases in heart rate or surges in brain activity. Physiological responses are recorded in the presence of a specific stimulus, such as a flashing light, or during a specific behavioral episode, such as a petit mal seizure. Standardized protocols are commonplace in psychophysiological assessment. Electronic equipment, such as electroencephalographs, electromyographs, and electrodermal measuring devices, are also common and require careful calibration. Psychophysiological assessment is a highly specialized area of behavioral assessment but is a powerful technology useful in diagnosing many disorders. This approach is not reviewed further here.

HISTORY TAKING: BEHAVIOR IN A LARGER, DEVELOPMENTAL CONTEXT

Behavior obviously occurs not in a vacuum, but rather in a multidimensional context. We have discussed the need to obtain behavior ratings and observations of children in more than one setting. Behavior often changes with a child's environment so issues of situationality and generalizability are important. In addition to its multidimensional context, another important context of behavior is the historical and developmental one. Child and salient family histories are frequently important, not only in diagnosis but also in decisions regarding specific interventions.

This fact is particularly apparent in the case of diagnosis. Without an adequate history, a child engaged in an appropriate grief reaction to a recent loss may be diagnosed as depressed. In fact, numerous disorders listed in the *Diagnostic and Statistical Manual of Mental Disorders,* 4th ed. (*DSM-IV;* APA, 1994) have many symptoms in common.

The diagnostic categories of ADHD and Posttraumatic Stress Disorder

(PTSD), for example, have approximately 13 symptoms in common. The majority of these 13 symptoms overlap with those of other anxiety disorders, and a considerable number overlap with Major Depressive Disorder and Bipolar Disorder, to name only a few. What often allows careful, accurate differentiation among these presentations is a comprehensive and detailed history of the child, his or her development, and to some extent the family (see also Coyle, Willis, Leber, & Culbertson, 1998). Differential diagnosis of these disorders is imperative, because treatments differ dramatically for some clients and misdiagnosis may lead to a worsening of the child's problems, violating the essential, prime directive of health service providers: *First, do no harm.*

A history may be the only way to determine whether a symptom or disorder is acute or chronic. The qualifications for many disorders stipulate that symptoms must be present for specific durations, such as 2 weeks or 1 month. These specifications appear in both medical (e.g., *DSM-IV*) and educational (e.g., Individuals with Disabilities Education Act [IDEA]) taxonomies of behavioral or emotional problems. For disorders that have clear developmental progressions, a history is essential to diagnosis and prognosis. A history can reveal fixations in development and allow caregivers to distinguish between functional and organic illnesses.

Collecting a family history along with a more specific, detailed history of the child's life gives a better view of the child's cultural context. The cultural context of the individual child is increasingly recognized as important both to diagnosis and to the development of an effective treatment plan (e.g., see Sandoval, Frisby, Geisenger, Scheuneman, & Grenier, 1998).

Practitioners can obtain a history through an interview or through a questionnaire. One well-designed questionnaire is the Structured Developmental History (SDH), a component of the BASC. The SDH is designed for administration (a) to high-functioning adults, (b) in a structured interview format for people who may not be able to complete the form independently, or (c) by practitioners who prefer the added opportunity to develop rapport afforded by the structured interview format.

The SDH can be an important element of any comprehensive evaluation of child and adolescent problems. This structured history provides a thorough review of social, psychological, developmental, educational, and medical information that may influence the diagnosis and treatment of a child. The information it provides is sometimes essential for differential diagnosis, and it also

DON'T FORGET

A practitioner can use the SDH as a *structured interview* with a parent or other caregiver, or a *questionnaire* that can be sent home for completion or filled out in the practitioner's office at school. When using the SDH as a questionnaire, the practitioner should review the completed form carefully in case clarification or elaboration is needed from the respondent.

may point to a need for referral to another professional. Not all of the information obtained in the SDH is relevant for every case, but some is always relevant.

The SDH is an attempt at detailed, wide-ranging coverage. Over 20 other history forms were reviewed in developing this instrument. It is designed to be useful in numerous settings, including clinics, schools, and hospitals.

The SDH Form

The sections of the SDH are sequenced in the order in which they often occur in a report, facilitating report writing for practitioners. Each section has a prominent heading, which enables the practitioner to skip to sections of interest or cross out sections that may be omitted (see Rapid Reference 1.2 for a listing of the sections).

The SDH begins by surveying fundamental information about the person

≋*Rapid Reference 1.2*

Section Headings of the BASC Structured Developmental History

1. Person Answering Questions	11. Birth
2. Referral Information	12. Development
3. Parents	13. Medical History
4. Primary Caregivers	14. Family Health
5. Child Care	15. Friendships
6. Family History	16. Recreation/Interests
7. Brothers/Sisters	17. Behavior/Temperament
8. Child's Residence	18. Adaptive Skills
9. Family Relations	19. Educational History
10. Pregnancy	20. Additional Comments

answering the questions and the reasons for bringing the child for services. In the clinic or private office, this information is crucial to formulating an assessment plan. If the individual referring a child is someone other than the respondent or a primary caregiver such as a teacher, counselor, or pediatrician, the practitioner should ascertain the parent's or caregiver's understanding of the referral information. Why does this caregiver think a referral was recommended, or alternatively, why has the caregiver initiated the referral process?

The SDH next calls for demographic, educational, and vocational data about the parents. The SDH also has sections for information on primary caregivers and child care, because the child may live not with parents, but perhaps with grandparents or foster parents. Moreover, a substantial portion of the child's day may be spent with yet another caregiver.

The next sections focus on family history, brothers and sisters, the child's residence, and family relations, including general activities, educational goals, and disciplinary practices. A knowledge of parental expectations and philosophy regarding education and discipline is useful in devising interventions and in communicating with parents.

The history of the pregnancy and birth may uncover problems of etiological significance. The relative difficulty and complexity of these events can affect the family's interactions with the child and thus influence behavior. The mother's use of medications and illicit substances during pregnancy may be important to ascertain; even legal substances such as alcohol or tobacco can have relevance to a presentation. Subtle problems, often overlooked, may also have implications for understanding current referral questions. For example, a mother may have experienced prolonged emotional distress during her pregnancy and may not mention the distress in an interview.

The SDH asks the respondent about milestones in development. The age of basic motor and language skill acquisition varies considerably. A consistent delay in overall skill development or a serious gap between motor and language development is noteworthy because such uneven maturation may persist.

Parents often have difficulty recalling early developmental events, particularly if they have two or more children. Parents can provide a more accurate and complete developmental history if they bring along the child's baby book or other records. Occasionally, a pediatrician's records are useful and can be requested; these records also provide information on the child's illnesses.

A normative framework is useful in evaluating the acquisition of various developmental milestones and other salient early behaviors. Tables 1.1–1.3 re-

Table 1.1 Common Developmental Milestones of the First Year of Life

Accomplishment	Age in Months[a]
Follows moving object with eyes or head	1
Laughs	3
Lifts head when prone	3
Grasps rattle	4
Puts hands together	4
Reaches for object	5
Smiles spontaneously	5
Rolls over on own	7
Places some weight on legs	8
Feeds self with fingers	8
Looks for objects not in plain sight	8
Transfers object from hand to hand	8
Turns to voice	8
Works for toy out of reach	9
Crawls	10
Pulls self to standing	10
Sits without support	10
Sits alone	11
Bangs object held in hands	12

[a]Age at which 90% of children can perform activity.

view many key behavioral accomplishments of a child's first six years. The tables provide a behavioral descriptor and the estimated age at which 9 out of 10 children perform the action consistently. These tables, brought together here from development texts and infant test items, provide a ready reference for reviewing key developmental events.

A medical history may shed light on the child's current status, provide information relevant to etiology, influence treatment recommendations, or

Table 1.2 Common Developmental Milestones of the Second and Third Years of Life

Accomplishment	Age in Months[a]
Says "mama" or "dada" specific to parent	13
Stands briefly	13
Walks holding on	13
Indicates wants (not crying)	14
Stands alone well	14
Stoops and gets up on own	14
Walks on own	14
Drinks from cup	17
Builds tower of 2 blocks	20
Says 3 words other than "mama" or "dada"	21
Takes off clothes	22
Points to 1 named body part	23
Kicks ball forward	24
Uses spoon, spilling little	24
Walks up steps, 1 at a time	24
Combines 2 words	28
Names 1 picture	30
Throws ball overhand	31
Counts 3 objects correctly	36
Jumps in place	36
Knows age and sex	36
Pedals tricycle	36

[a]Age at which 90% of children can perform activity.

Table 1.3 Common Developmental Milestones of the Fourth, Fifth, and Sixth Years of Life

Accomplishment	Age in Months[a]
Uses plural words	38
Copies circle	40
Dresses with supervision	42
Plays interactive games	42
Gives first and last name	46
Tells a story	48
Buttons clothing	50
Separates easily from mother	56
Hops on one foot	59
Copies triangle	60
Dresses without supervision	60
Heel to toe walks	60
Skips	60
Draws man with at least 3 distinguishable parts	62
Catches bounced ball	66
Copies square	72

[a]Age at which 90% of children can perform activity.

suggest the need for further assessments. In particular, a child with a history of prolonged high fever, meningitis, encephalitis, head injury, febrile seizures, or chronic use of psychoactive medications probably should undergo a comprehensive neuropsychological examination as well as psychological and behavioral assessments.

In addition to surveying past illnesses and injuries, the SDH asks about respiratory, cardiovascular, gastrointestinal, genitourinary, musculoskeletal, dermatological, neurological, and allergy problems. Such problems, if persistent, often have educational and psychological implications. Hearing and vision are also covered in the SDH. Even minor vision or hearing problems can lead to learning and behavior disorders. These problems often go undetected prior to the child's entrance in school. Interventions for such problems are necessary before any psychological strategies are attempted.

The SDH then requests information on any history of medical and psychological care the child has received, including specialty care such as neurological, psychiatric, or psychological exams. In addition, the family health history explores genetic, chromosomal, and high-risk health factors that may be relevant to diagnosis, referral, or treatment. If a broad category such as Mental Illness, Physical Handicaps, Nervousness, Behavior Disorder, Emotional Disturbance, or Other Learning Problems is marked *yes,* the practitioner should ask follow-up questions.

Next, the history form gathers information on friendships and recreational interests, followed by information about behavior, temperament, and fundamental adaptive skills. A quick screen of behavioral disposition and adaptive behavior can often highlight areas for more thorough assessment.

Educational history is the last content section on the SDH. Schooling, as the major structured component of a child's life, greatly influences socialization and psychological development. Changing schools often may have a substantial impact on a child.

Of more than 600 neurodegenerative diseases now identified, most have or are suspected to have a genetic or chromosomal basis. Some, such as Huntington's disease, are generally considered to be disorders of adulthood but may show their first manifestations in childhood. Often the first indications of a neurodegenerative condition may be symptoms viewed as psychological or neuropsychological rather than physical. Thus, without a good history, these disorders may be misdiagnosed. The SDH does not list every genetic disorder, but it does highlight several relatively high-frequency conditions and ask about their occurrence in family members.

Some disorders, such as schizophrenia, bipolar disorder, and depression, have uncertain etiologies and may or may not be genetic. If there is a family history of their occurrence, a clearer diagnosis of these conditions may be possible. When the SDH does not specifically list a disorder, the respondent may note it in more general categories such as Mental Illness. In these cases, follow-up questioning by the clinician is necessary to pinpoint the disorder.

For a child undergoing a psychopharmacological intervention, a careful history is useful in detecting undesirable effects of medication. Tics and habit spasms, for example, may be a problem for many children. These *adverse effects,* popularly known as *side effects,* can occur in conjunction with a stimulant or with antidepressant therapy for ADHD. A family history can help to differentiate among related clinical disorders, the onset of a new disorder, and undesirable effects of a treatment regimen.

Both medical and psychosocial aspects of a family can potentially influence the presentation of a child seen for psychological or educational testing. Without a careful structured history such as that obtained with the SDH, a practitioner may overlook many disorders as diagnostic possibilities.

TEST YOURSELF

1. Behavioral assessment is a way of thinking that

(a) relies on a specific set of tests and procedures.

(b) acknowledges only observable, overt behavior.

(c) makes use of assessments to form hypotheses about behavior.

(d) makes use of assessments to form hypotheses about the structure of disorders.

2. What forms of behavior does contemporary behavioral assessment include?

(a) Only observable, overt behavior

(b) Overt behavior and covert thoughts, feelings, and desires

(c) Overt behavior; covert thoughts, feelings, and desires; and long-standing traits such as anxiety

(d) Overt behavior; covert thoughts, feelings, and desires; long-standing traits such as anxiety; and deep-seated, psychodynamic conflicts

3. Behaviorally oriented practitioners

(a) use the traditional clinical interview and problem definition.

(b) eschew clinical interviewing, which gives unquantifiable results.

(c) omit any reference to covert thoughts, feelings, and desires when defining the presenting problem.

(d) focus on problem solving, seek the antecedents of behavior, and define the presenting problem as a matter of specific actions.

4. Behavioral interviewers

    (a) identify a presenting problem but deemphasize the history of the problem.

    (b) identify a presenting problem, obtain its history and context, and include some developmental history.

    (c) identify a presenting problem, obtain its history and context, include some developmental history, and try to understand the client's view of the world.

    (d) focus primarily on the client's view of the world.

5. A behaviorally oriented practitioner

    (a) only identifies the presenting problem.

    (b) identifies and defines the presenting problem.

    (c) identifies the presenting problem, defines it, and seeks to determine the environmental events that accompany it.

    (d) identifies the presenting problem, defines it, and seeks to determine the social forces that maintain it.

6. When defining a client's presenting problem, a behaviorally oriented practitioner

    (a) develops a brief definition in one or two sentences.

    (b) designates target behaviors.

    (c) uses clinical terms.

    (d) describes it as the client would.

7. When defining a client's presenting problem, a behavioral practitioner emphasizes

    (a) transient psychological states.

    (b) transient states and enduring traits.

    (c) enduring traits and specific actions.

    (d) specific actions.

8. A behavioral practitioner develops a plan that includes

    (a) intervention, implementation of the intervention, evaluation of outcomes, and modification of the plan.

    (b) intervention, implementation of the intervention, evaluation of outcomes, and analysis of evaluation results.

    (c) implementation, evaluation of outcomes, and reporting of results to a teacher or caregiver.

    (d) implementation, collection of outcome data, and evaluation of outcomes.

(continued)

9. The advantages of behavioral interviewing include all except the following:

(a) It is useful in obtaining both general and specific information.

(b) The data obtained leads to a great deal of inference.

(c) It seeks out the current circumstances that trigger a behavior.

(d) It is an eminently practical approach.

10. The disadvantages of behavioral interviewing include all except the following:

(a) It lacks a standard protocol.

(b) Its reliability and validity are limited.

(c) The behavior assessed tends to remain the same over time.

(d) A lack of quantifiable outcomes limits research on this approach.

11. Broad-band behavior rating scales provide all of the following except

(a) an overall description of a child's behavior.

(b) results that are easily quantified.

(c) differential diagnosis among disorders.

(d) ratings from respondent who is known to be unbiased.

12. In direct observation, ratings are taken

(a) in a natural setting; when the behavior occurs; by impartial observers; and according to clear descriptions of behaviors.

(b) in a natural setting; when the behavior occurs; by self-report; and according to clear descriptions of behaviors.

(c) in a controlled setting; when the behavior occurs; by self-report; and according to quantifiable descriptions of behaviors.

(d) in a controlled setting; retrospectively; by self-report; and according to quantifiable descriptions of behaviors.

13. A history form, such as the Structured Developmental History, can help the practitioner to distinguish

(a) chronic disorders from acute ones.

(b) depression from an ordinary grief reaction.

(c) disorders with many symptoms in common.

(d) all of the above.

Answers: 1. c; 2. c; 3. d; 4. b; 5. c; 6. b; 7. d; 8. a; 9. b; 10. c; 11. d; 12. a; 13. d

Two

MERITS OF THE INVENTORIES

I n this chapter we assess the practical and technical merits of the BASC, the CBCL, and the CRS-R, using nontechnical language when possible. For each inventory, we present practical merits followed by technical ones. Here, practical merits include such considerations as brevity and ease of administration. Technical merits include such statistical considerations as the development, reliability, and validity of the inventories. The following paragraphs explain the latter two terms. An explanation of test development itself is outside the scope of this book. Ramsay and Reynolds (2000a), however, describe this process in a readable style.

RELIABILITY AND VALIDITY

We turn first to two fundamental statistical concepts. In everyday language, *reliability* refers to the consistency of scores obtained from a test. A study supporting reliability of one type or another might show that a test's results are consistent over time, in several geographic regions, or for children of both sexes. *Validity* refers to the accuracy of interpretations made from performance on a test; such performance is typically expressed in the form of scores (see Rapid Reference 2.1).

Practitioners should be aware of two characteristics of validity. First, only performance can support the validity of an interpretation; a test itself cannot. Indeed, only performance can provide information about an examinee, suggest an intervention, or help to monitor progress. The test itself performs none of these functions. It is only a few sheets of paper. Thus, validity is a characteristic of the interpretation of test performance.

Therefore, a good question to ask when selecting a test might be, "If I interpret the scores on this test as reflecting anxiety, how valid will my interpre-

===Rapid Reference 2.1

Definitions

Reliability refers to the consistency of scores obtained from a test. A study supporting reliability of one type or another might show that a test's results are consistent over time, across several regions, or for children of both sexes.

Validity refers to the accuracy of interpretations of test performance; such performance is typically expressed in the form of scores.

Construct validity traditionally refers to the accuracy of the association of test scores and interpretation of these scores with some underlying trait or construct that is thought to be associated with the test and its requirements of the examinee.

tation be?" This is not to say that validity is only or even chiefly a practitioner's responsibility. Test developers suggest interpretations; researchers challenge, refine, and supplement these interpretations. People in either field must provide evidence that any interpretation they suggest has satisfactory validity and must be accurate and honest in reporting how much validity an interpretation may have. A practitioner then considers these suggested interpretations, examines information from other sources, and develops interpretations of an individual examinee's behavior.

A second notable characteristic of validity is that it holds true only for a specific group and purpose. Scores that lead to highly valid interpretations when used to diagnose Conduct Disorder in White males 10 years of age, for example, may have little validity when used to diagnose Antisocial Personality Disorder in older, Black females, and still less validity when distractibility is the condition being assessed. These characteristics of validity are related in that the purposes suggested for a test lead to specific interpretations of its results (AERA, APA, & NCME, 1999; Rapid Reference 2.2).

===Rapid Reference 2.2

Defining Validity

The new Standards for Educational and Psychological Testing (American Educational Research Association; AERA, American Psychological Association; APA, & National Council on Measurement in Education; NCME, 1999) define validity as *the degree to which evidence and theory support the interpretations of test scores entailed by proposed uses of tests.*

Construct Validity

Later chapters of this book refer to one type of validity, so we briefly define this concept here. Anastasi (1988) defines *construct validity* as the extent to which test scores measure a theoretical characteristic or other theoretical construct. During test development, the author of the test defines a construct, such as writing aptitude, depression, or hyperactivity. The author might ask questions such as these: What is hyperactivity? How would a hyperactive child behave? What tasks might this child have trouble completing? What would the child do differently from one with a different condition, for example, anxiety? The answers become part of an elaborate definition based on actual behaviors and experiences that a person might have (Kaplan & Saccuzzo, 1997; Kubiszin & Borich, 1996; Ramsay & Reynolds, 2000a).

Tests are designed to measure this construct as it is defined. In the above example, then, any evidence that the test is identifying children who are hyperactive according to the author's elaborate definition supports construct validity. Evidence that the definition is correct also supports construct validity, and both types of evidence are indispensable to support validity of this sort (Kaplan & Saccuzzo, 1997; Kubiszin & Borich, 1996; Ramsay & Reynolds, 2000a). Construct validity is a complex and sweeping notion. Indeed, all other forms of validity are aspects of this one. For a more rigorous definition of construct validity, see Rapid Reference 2.1. For other types of validity, such as *content validity*, see Anastasi (1988) or Kaplan and Saccuzzo (1997).

Convergent and Discriminant Validity

A study supporting validity might show that an attention scale identifies adolescents diagnosed with ADHD. A study showing that this same test does not identify psychotic or anxious adolescents would also provide support for the validity of its suggested interpretation as a measure of attention problems. The first example has to do with *convergent* validity, and the second, with *discriminant* validity. Construct validity—and therefore all validity—is sometimes divided into these two types.

Convergent validity is the extent to which test scores are related to what they are meant to measure. Conversely, discriminant validity is the extent to which test scores are not related to what they are not meant to measure. A study might show that inner-city children's scores on an attention scale identify respondents who have been diagnosed with ADHD. These results would support convergent validity. The study might also show that these scores do not identify children with depressive or anxious symptoms. Taken together, both of these findings would support discriminant validity.

Moreover, even the results for depression would support the suggested interpretation of test scores as reflecting attention problems. This is so because, if an attentional interpretation is valid, scores on a test should be more closely related to attentional problems than to some other construct such as depression. On the other hand, a study may produce low validity figures both for attention problems and for depression. In this case, an attentional interpretation would have little validity after all.

The ideas of reliability and validity are central to an understanding of the quality and applications of any standardized test. Having introduced these two concepts, we now incorporate them into an evaluation of the three most widely used checklist inventories.

THE BASC

Practical Merits of the BASC

According to numerous independent reviewers, the BASC has several advantages over its older competitors. Item development involved both questioning teachers to survey their concerns about students and surveying students' concerns about the behaviors exhibited by their peers. The resulting system, particularly those scales that refer to the school and the classroom, is highly relevant in actual practice, possessing a degree of documented social validity not often seen in behavior rating scales. In addition, some items are independently interpretable as well as being parts of their respective scales and composites.

The BASC subscales were derived using a combination of rational, theoretical, and empirical methods, in contrast to the purely actuarial approach of the CBCL. BASC scales and items thus have a high degree of concordance with other diagnostic systems and with the scientific literature on child development and psychopathology.

Another advantage of the BASC is its main composites. Two of them, Externalizing Problems and Internalizing Problems, are supported by copious research on the two concepts. The third, Adaptive Skills, is not as well established, but its centrality in any setting can hardly be disputed. In addition, the measurement of resilience factors and other adaptive characteristics is both important and current. An extensive accounting for adaptiveness is unique to the BASC among widely used checklist inventories. In fact, behavior rating scales have been roundly criticized for failing to measure beneficial traits. The BASC is the first and thus far the only set of scales to remedy this problem, devoting multiple subscales to positive behavioral attributes.

The BASC scales have one manual rather than several. The manual is easy to understand, and sections repeated for child, parent, and teacher rating scales make the instructions easy to follow and learn. An additional advantage of the BASC is the extensive information provided through relatively simple calculations: 14 subscales, as well as validity scales and composites.

The BASC is the only instrument reviewed that provides the user with a choice of same-sex or combined-sex norm tables. Other scales force the user invariably to use one or the other, and the diagnostic outcomes may differ. The CBCL and the CRS-R offer only same-sex normative data. The multiple BASC norm reference groups permit comparisons between the examinee and others of the same age and gender, as well as to the general age cohort. A set of clinical norms is also available, allowing additional comparisons to known diagnostic groups. The CBCL offers clinical norms, whereas the CRS-R does not.

The BASC components yielding standardized or scaled scores—that is, the three levels of the TRS and PRS and the two levels of the SRP—all contain dissimulation scales. *Dissimulation* is the act of misrepresenting one's own or another person's thoughts, feelings, or behavior. It may occur for a variety of reasons. A teacher may rate a child as exceptionally aggressive and disturbed in an attempt to have the child removed from the class. A parent may engage in the same behavior to gain excess damages in a lawsuit, qualification for Social Security disability income, or a special service or exemption for the child. A teenager may not want the examiner or practitioner to know about troubling thoughts or feelings and may deny common problems, especially alcohol or drug abuse.

The BASC contains validity scales designed to detect such responses. The F (Infrequency) Scale detects exaggeration of problems and the L (Lie or Social Desirability) Scale detects minimization of problems. A separate V (Validity) Scale detects invalid responding such as that which may occur if the respondent cannot or does not read the items before answering, or if the examinee responds randomly or flippantly. While useful in many contexts,

DON'T FORGET

Of the three major behavior rating scales, only the BASC contains sub-scales designed to detect dissimulation and inconsistent responding. This makes the BASC especially useful in legal proceedings.

such scales are especially important in legal settings in which forensic examinations are common and the examinee or rater has something tangible to gain as a result of a particular score pattern. Any of the BASC computer scoring programs flag unreliable or inconsistent responding to highly similar items, but the Consistency Index is not available for hand scoring.

Another feature of the BASC that is unique among the scales in this volume is the presence of *critical items* on each BASC form. These items, derived both rationally and empirically, have particularly high levels of social and clinical validity. For the most part, they represent thoughts, feelings, or behaviors that reflect serious issues such as self-harm, or thoughts, behaviors, and feelings that are out of control. The BASC format highlights these responses on the hand-scored record form and prints them on the front of the printout of the computer-scored version. As a result, clinicians can easily recognize and follow up on the items marked.

With regard to reading and linguistic concerns, the BASC SRP-C, SRP-A, and PRS have very low reading levels. A Flesch-Kincaid analysis reported in the manual sets the reading level of these scales at Grades 2.0, 3.0, and 2.0, respectively. Rapid Reference 2.3 provides readability estimates for all forms of

≡Rapid Reference 2.3

Readability Estimates of BASC Forms[a]

Scale	Readability Grade Level
Self-Report of Personality–Child	2.0
Self-Report of Personality–Adolescent	3.0
Teacher Rating Scale	not rated
Parent Rating Scale	2.0

[a]Obtained using the Flesch-Kincaid index.

the BASC. Spanish-language versions of the BASC PRS are also available. These were designed with tryout and input from the major Hispanic populations in the United States: Puerto Ricans, Mexican Americans, and Cuban Americans. This process continued *iteratively*—that is, repeating again and again as long as further improvement was detected—until respondents from all three groups reported that the translation was easy to read and understand. Finally, each BASC form is available for online administration and scoring via the BASC Plus computer program, and each has hand-score, computer entry, and scannable versions.

The chief disadvantage of the BASC is its newness, resulting in a paucity of postpublication research assessing the validity of the recommended interpretations of the various BASC scales. Given the newness of the BASC, some practitioners may consider the manual bold in some of the interpretations it suggests, relying as it does upon content validity and general support from the scientific literature. Extensive prepublication results are available, however, from research involving more than 33,000 children, parents, and teachers. High levels of concurrent and discriminant validity were found. In addition, postpublication studies have appeared, and the ensuing paragraphs describe several of them.

Technical Merits of the BASC

The norming sample of the BASC includes more than 19,000 young people, greatly exceeding the sample sizes of all similar tests. Thus, researchers can study small groups of young people who have too little representation to be included in studies of many other tests. In turn, clinicians can potentially use the BASC with these groups. The size of the norming sample, along with the sampling plan used in the BASC's development—called *population-proportionate stratified random sampling*—ensures not only representative norms, but very high stability of the parameter estimates needed to derive norm reference tables. No other rating scale offers a norming sample that approaches the size and quality found with the BASC. In addition, such large amounts of data collected during the BASC's development have allowed the authors to eliminate and modify items and scales not only through traditional psychometrics, but also on the basis of feedback from numerous teachers, children, parents, and clinicians.

The BASC manual (Reynolds & Kamphaus, 1998) provides extensive psychometric information. Data regarding internal consistency reliability are most frequently good ($\alpha \geq .80$) or very good ($\alpha \geq .90$). Similarly, median test-retest reliabilities across a 2- to 8-week time period are reported as .89 for the preschool rating scales, .91 for the child rating scales, and .82 for the adolescent rating scales; see Rapid Reference 2.4 for more detail. The manual also provides internal consistency estimates by age level and form (Table 12.1, page 102). Median reliability estimates are reported as .82 for the preschool rating scales, .86 for the child rating scales, and .90 for the adolescent rating scales. Comparable reliabilities (.84, .82, and .85, respectively) are reported for clinical samples at these age levels. These values all represent the BASC TRS for illustration, but PRS data are highly comparable; see Chapter 13 of the BASC manual, beginning on page 129. Data for the BASC SRP appear in Chapter 14 of the manual, and these data are extensive as well.

As previously noted, the BASC is the newest of the three scales reviewed in this volume and consequently has less postpublication research supporting its validity. The amount of validity data presented in the BASC manual (Reynolds & Kamphaus, 1998), however, greatly exceeds that of other scales. The item and scale organization of the BASC, for example, was derived from theoretical and rational premises, and then was tested empirically using covariance structure analysis (CSA). This procedure allows the theoretical underpinnings of a scale to guide the development process, but requires an empirical or actuarial fit that maximizes both reliability and validity. Subsequently, experienced

≡Rapid Reference 2.4

Test-Retest Reliability of the BASC Teacher Rating Scales

BASC TRS subscales have very high test-retest reliability over a period of 2 to 8 weeks. Every subscale has a test-retest reliability coefficient of .70 or higher, except the Somatization scale at the *child* age level (.59). Median values for the preschool, child, and adolescent rating scales are .89, .91, and .82, respectively. Complete test-retest reliability information for the BASC TRS can be found in the manual in Table 12.4 (p. 105). Over a 7-month period, the median scale correlation drops to .69, but half the scales remain at .70 or higher. The Atypicality scale has the lowest test-retest correlation over the 7-month time frame. PRS data are highly comparable.

clinicians in the field of childhood psychopathology sorted scales and items; their suggestions closely matched the empirical results of the CSA.

Throughout the BASC manual, reports are presented showing extensive concurrent validity data between BASC scales and numerous other instruments, including self-report inventories; traditional scales such as the Personality Inventory for Children; and other behavior rating scales, including the CBCL and the CRS. Comparably named scales tended to correlate highest in each analysis. When compared with CBCL and CRS subtests, the BASC scales correlated highest with like-named subtests, particularly on the CBCL (see Rapid Reference 2.5).

The BASC manual also reports clinical group differentiation, presenting T-score profiles for eight different clinical or diagnostic groups for all BASC forms. The BASC shows very good sensitivity and specificity in differentiating among these groups. For definitions of sensitivity and specificity, see the section on the CBCL below.

The BASC and Attention-Deficit/Hyperactivity Disorder

Although ethnic and gender differences allow for various interpretations, a test that distinguishes a particular disorder from its absence always has some evidence support-

≡*Rapid Reference 2.5*

Correlations of BASC Scales with CBCL and CRS Scales

The BASC shows moderate correlations with similar scales on the CBCL and the CRS. Correlations are consistently higher between the BASC and the CBCL than between the BASC and the CRS.

DON'T FORGET

The BASC Manual provides data on BASC profiles and on differentiation from normal children for the following clinical groups:

- Conduct Disorder
- Behavior Disorder (unspecified type)
- Major Depressive Disorder
- Autism
- ADHD
- Learning Disability (unspecified type)
- Mild Mental Retardation
- Emotionally Disturbed (under the IDEA definition)

ing its usefulness as a test for that disorder. Nation (1996) tested the BASC's ability to identify young people with ADHD. The scales tested included Anxiety and Depression on the SRP-C, and Aggression, Anxiety, Attention Problems, Conduct Problems, Depression, and Hyperactivity on the PRS-C. Individual items did not always perform satisfactorily, but all scales showed statistically significant differences for control versus ADHD participants. Nation concluded that the BASC is representative of ADHD symptomatology.

Vaughn, Riccio, Hynd, and Hall (1997) compared the accuracy (i.e., sensitivity and specificity) of the BASC and the CBCL for diagnoses of ADHD. They concluded that both scales were quite good at detecting the presence of ADHD (sensitivity) but noted that the BASC had better predictive validity for children who did not meet the criteria for a diagnosis of ADHD (specificity); the BASC more accurately detected normalcy. When subtypes of ADHD were examined, the BASC showed a clear advantage over the CBCL, especially for the ADHD Predominantly Inattentive Type. With regard to accurate identification of children as having or not having ADHD, Ostrander, Weinfurt, Yarnold, and August (1998) confirmed the Vaughn et al. finding and noted that the BASC was more accurate than the CBCL overall. Nevertheless, the Ostrander et al. (1998) results on correct classification of ADHD subtypes were contradictory to those of Vaughn et al., implying that the CBCL is more accurate at identifying the ADHD Predominantly Inattentive Type. Clearly, more research is needed to clarify this issue.

The BASC and Demographic Variables: Gender, Race, and Socioeconomic Status (SES)

Dunbar (1999) analyzed for gender differences on the BASC Externalizing composites: Attention, Conduct Problems, and Hyperactivity. The participants were 3,343 children, aged 6–11 years, from the norming sample; 2,084 completed the PRS-C, and 1,259 completed the TRS-C. The researcher used partial correlations and the Johnson-Neyman technique.

Partial correlations identified many more items than the Johnson-Neyman technique as showing a difference, typically *male > female*. Dunbar (1999) noted that partial correlations have a high Type I error rate and assume a linear regression line, which none of the Externalizing items show. Thus, partial correlations may have overidentified gender differences. Items showing higher scores by males may reflect real gender differences rather than bias. Analysis for scale differences did not reveal any statistically significant differences by gender. The analysis did, however, produce reliabilities of .84–.92.

Knight (1996) analyzed data for the BASC norming sample of more than 19,000 children aged 4–18 years. This study utilized PRS data for 3,210 children in the general sample: 2,887 Whites and 337 African Americans. Hispanics ($n = 178$) and other racial or ethnic categories ($n = 81$) were not included. Participants were divided into two groups of 1,605 children each to test reliability using Analysis of Covariance (ANCOVA) and partial correlations.

The researcher then tested four variables: the common factor, gender, race, and SES. Each was partialed in those analyses in which it was not being tested. The common factor served only as a partialed variable. Therefore, Knight (1996) made separate comparisons for age groups 4–5, 6–11, 12–18, and for the two groups of 1,605 children. Table 2.1 presents results for both of these groups. The results for gender, race, and SES are all likely to reflect real differences across groups rather than effects of test bias, given present findings on the BASC.

Extensive analyses to assess potential cultural biases in the BASC were undertaken during scale development (see Reynolds & Kamphaus, 1998) and have been extended since that time (e.g., Mayfield & Reynolds, 1998). Each stage of item and scale development incorporated judgmental and statistical evaluations of cultural bias. In the final published version, items that showed differential item functioning (DIF) as a function of race or ethnicity had been eliminated. Postpublication analyses of the potential for ethnic bias in the BASC revealed no meaningful effects on errors in diagnosis attributable to ethnic bias (Mayfield & Reynolds, 1998).

None of the other rating scales reviewed here have undergone the pre- and postpublication scrutiny of the BASC with regard to potential biasing factors in its application. The various differences in scores across groups on the BASC appear to reflect real differences in behavior and not artifacts of measurement. Knowledge of the pattern and magnitude of such group differences is useful in scale interpretation (e.g., see Reynolds & Kamphaus, 1998). The BASC scales, however, appear to be interpretable first as measures of their respective constructs, such as depression, rather than as measures affected principally by cultural variation.

Table 2.1 Statistically Significant Differences on BASC Scales Common to Both Groups

Age Group	Analysis	Differences[a]	Higher Scorers
		Between Genders	
4–5	Both	None in either sample	—
6–11	ANCOVA	Dep, Withdraw	F
	Semipartial r's	Agg, Conduct	M
		Anx, Dep, Withdraw	F
12–18	ANCOVA	Anx, Dep	F
		Attn	M
	Semipartial r's	Anx, Dep	F
		Agg, Conduct, Attn, Soc[b]	M
		Between Racial Groups	
4–5	Both	None common to both samples	—
6–11	ANCOVA	Agg, Dep	W
	Semipartial r's	Agg, Dep	W
12–18	ANCOVA	Atyp	B
	Semipartial r's	Atyp	B
		Between SES Groups	
4–5	Both	None common to both samples	—
6–11	ANCOVA	Lead	Low SES[c]
	Semipartial r's	Lead, Soc	Low SES[c]
12–18	ANCOVA	Agg	Low SES
	Semipartial r's	Lead	Low SES[c]

Note. Dep = Depression, Withdraw = Withdrawal, Agg = Aggression, Conduct = Conduct Problems, Anx = Anxiety, Attn = Attention Problems, Atyp = Atypicality, Lead = Leadership, Soc = Social Skills.

[a]Statistically significant differences common to both samples tested.

[b]Males obtained better Social Skills scores.

[c]Low SES children obtained better scores for the specified scales(s).

THE CBCL

Practical Merits of the CBCL

The CBCL has a number of advantages for examiners. The items are alphabetized, reducing the opportunity to guess the meanings of the items, which would render them less accurate. Clinicians do not need to calculate T scores; the profile layout allows them to read across from the graphic profile to a column of T scores. The administration instructions found in the manual are brief and clear. Finally, the manuals for the CBCL and related instruments are very similar and thereby facilitate learning.

Achenbach's (1991a) two broadband scales, Externalizing Problems and Internalizing Problems, are another advantage. As noted earlier for the BASC, these constructs have copious support in the scientific literature. A Young Adult Self-Report (YASR) also is available for ages 18–30. Finally, some practitioners see the number and variety of checklists offered as an advantage.

A disadvantage of the CBCL is its scoring, which is complex in comparison with that of other checklist inventories and which requires considerable familiarity with the manual. Parts of the manuals and supporting materials are badly organized, so desired material may be hard to find. In addition, some of the text may be difficult to understand, particularly passages addressing the technical aspects of test development.

Like most instruments in widespread, long-standing use, the CBCL has received its share of unflattering commentary. In a recent study, Goodman and Scott (1999) made several unfavorable comparisons with Goodman's Strengths and Difficulties Questionnaire, noting also the similarities between the two instruments. Both tests are available in many languages. Both enjoy widespread use in clinical and educational practice and in clinical, developmental, and epidemiological research.

The two tests differ, however, in several respects (Goodman & Scott, 1999). The CBCL is considerably longer, its psychopathology scales consist entirely of negatively worded items, and some of its items have no conceptual link to their respective scales. Eiraldi, Power, Karustis, and Goldstein (2000) have also critiqued the CBCL, noting that it has one scale covering both depression and anxiety, whereas other tests, such as the BASC and the Devereux Scales of Mental Disorders, have a separate scale for each of the two constructs. The single scale is both an advantage and a disadvantage. The CBCL scale has less diagnostic utility but more ease and speed of administration.

Technical Merits of the CBCL

The norming sample for the CBCL (Achenbach, 1991a) included 2,368 children and adolescents—a somewhat small sample, considering that it was divided into a number of ethnic, age, and other groups. The age ranges used were 4–5, 6–11, and 12–18 years. Participants represented 52 settings in the United States. Although 75% were Caucasian, socioeconomic status was well represented. The sample comprised matched clinical and nonclinical samples.

Achenbach (1991a) investigated the reliability or *consistency* of the CBCL over a week, on average. Reliabilities were very high. Reliabilities over a longer period, such as six months or a year, were necessary so that, in later clinical applications, any difference in a young person's performance over time could be attributed to changes in the person's behavior, not to an unreliable test. Reliabilities over 1 year and over 2 years were the object of another investigation (Achenbach). Table 2.2 presents the scales that showed good reliability over 1 year for respondents tested at 6 and 7 years and for those tested at 7 and 8 years. Table 2.3 presents the scales showing good reliability over 2 years with respondents tested at 6 and 8 years of age. Here, good reliability of scores is defined as ≥ .70.

The CBCL can, however, be criticized on statistical grounds. This inventory was developed primarily using principal components analysis (PCA) and principal factor analysis. CBCL items provide only three *response options* or possible

Table 2.2 CBCL Scales Showing Good ($r \geq .70$) Test-Retest Reliability over One Year

	Age in Years	
Scale	6, 7	7, 8
Withdrawn	.79	.75
Attention Problems	.71	.77
Aggressive Behavior	.84	.87
Internalizing	.75	.82
Externalizing	.87	.86
Total score	.84	.86

Table 2.3 CBCL Scales Showing Good (*r* ≥ .70) Test-Retest Reliability over Two Years

Scale	Pearson *r*
Social Problems	.71
Attention Problems	.75
Aggressive Behavior	.87
Internalizing	.70
Externalizing	.86
Total score	.71

answers. Most scales, including the BASC and the CRS, provide four. Items with few response options often generate coarse, approximate measurement, which can distort the results of factor analyses and related techniques such as PCA (Heubeck, 2000).

Achenbach (1991a) used *varimax rotation* in developing the CBCL. This procedure assumes that the subscales are independent (uncorrelated with each other). In direct contrast, Dedrick, Greenbaum, Friedman, Wetherington, and Knoff (1997) found that the scales—or, to be correct, the scores obtained on them—correlated with each other. The correlations ranged from .193 between Delinquent Behavior and Somatic Complaints to .820 between Thought Problems and Attention Problems. These results were similar to those reported by Achenbach.

Achenbach (1991a) included five items on two or three subscales each. Neither Dedrick et al. (1997) nor Heubeck (2000) found much support for these item placements. Heubeck reported that all five of the items discriminated poorly between conditions. Dedrick et al. reported that four of them were below Achenbach's cutoff designated for correlations with the eight factors.

The CBCL development process emphasized factor analysis over theory. As a result, researchers have questioned the item content of some of the scales. Some items have no clear conceptual link with their respective scales (Doyle, Ostrander, Skare, Crosby, & August, 1997). Although such disconnections are often regarded as a limitation, their actual advantages and disadvantages are matters for scientific study. Tests of some behaviors, such as alcohol and drug abuse, consist entirely of *subtle items,* items whose meaning the examinee cannot guess. The test developer selects these items to avert any attempt by examinees to conceal their true behavior.

The CBCL and Odds Ratios

The CBCL manual (Achenbach, 1991a) presents odds ratios (OR), the ratio of two groups' odds of having a condition when one group has a particular risk factor. The manual shows two groups' odds of scoring in the clinical range on a CBCL scale when one group has been referred. A better approach would be to show the reverse: two groups' odds of being in the referred group when one group scores above a designated score. This is so because the goal of the analysis is to evaluate the test as a predictor. In this case, referred status is the *criterion* or predicted variable. The direction of a prediction is from predictor to criterion—here, from score to referral. Reporting that is consistent with this direction would be clearer and more understandable.

Furthermore, an OR denotes the association between a variable and the odds of another variable. A correlation coefficient, such as Pearson's r, denotes the association between the variables themselves. Here, the association entails a specific subtest and referral status, not the odds of either variable. Thus, r is an appropriate estimate. A simple measure called d (*difference*) is also appropriate (Ramsay, 2000; Ramsay & Reynolds, 2000b).

The correlations for Withdrawn and Somatic Complaints were $r = .66$ and $r = .52$, respectively. The difference between them was .14. The corresponding ORs were 11.6 and 11.5, a very small difference. The Pearson correlations of Social and School Competence were $r = .73$ and $r = .87$, another .14 difference. The ORs were 23.9 and 116.5, the latter figure being the largest in the table. Thus, an identical difference between Pearson correlations accompanied a much larger difference between ORs. The two measures behaved quite differently in this example. In addition, the r's correlating referral status with Delinquent Behavior and with Aggressive Behavior were highly similar at $r = .77$ and $r = .78$. The ORs were considerably different at 40.2 and 28.0.

ORs are often much larger than a corresponding r or d statistic, so they commonly lead to exaggerated interpretations of research findings. Researchers who report ORs at all should also report the odds themselves, in addition to a measure such as r or d. In some domains of epidemiological research, ORs reported alone often find their way into news reports. The resulting story is as misleading as it is dramatic: People who take medicine X, eat food Y, or wear sunscreen Z have, for example, ten times the risk of some serious illness.

Unknown to the reader, this increased risk may still be small, perhaps 1% or even much less. The correlation between the sunscreen and illness may also be small. Actual odds and an r or d value would flag the small findings (Ramsay, 2000; Ramsay & Reynolds, 2000b). Such reporting may be one reason, perhaps the major reason, that many foods and chemicals seem to be dangerous as portrayed in news reports.

Researchers in psychological and educational measurement must not reproduce this misuse of statistics. Epidemiology canvasses large regions and populations, whereas assessment focuses on the individual client. A statistic that is apt for one field may be unsuited to the other. We suggest that practitioners who see ORs reported should view them with much caution. If r's are also reported, interpret them instead. If only ORs are reported, disregard them. Fortunately, Achenbach (1991a) has presented r's alongside ORs, permitting a meaningful interpretation.

Statistical Significance and Effect Size

The manual (Achenbach, 1991a) sometimes stresses statistical significance. This practice is unadvisable, especially in testing, because significance of this sort is typically present even when reliability and validity correlations are too small to be even remotely satisfactory. The problem becomes acute with larger sample sizes. Most discussions on reliability and validity can omit statistical significance entirely.

A related issue is *effect size,* the size or strength of an association (Ramsay, 2000; Ramsay & Reynolds, 2000b). The manual (Achenbach, 1991a) notes correctly that $r = .59$ indicates a large association according to Cohen (1988). It is not considered large, however, when test scores are being evaluated for reliability or for most types of validity. More common standards are .80 and sometimes .90.

The Cross-Informant Model

An important development with the 1991 revisions of the CBCL is eight *cross-informant* scales consisting of 85 total items. The factors originally measured by the inventory varied for different age and sex groups, making interpretation difficult. Thus, Achenbach (1991a, 1991b, 1991c) used principal component analysis to derive *core syndromes,* sets of items that were common to most age and sex combinations. A cross-informant syndrome was one made up of items from the core syndromes as they appeared in at least two of the three CBCL protocols. These syndromes, then, would be consistent both for sex and age combinations and for CBCL protocols. A study by Heubeck (2000) suggests that they may be consistent in different countries as well. Exploratory factor-analytic techniques lend support to the cross-informant scales (Brown & Achenbach, 1993).

Dedrick et al. (1997) conducted a confirmatory factor analysis with 631 participants aged 8–18 years. All participants were identified as having serious emotional disturbances; most were White (72.7%) and male (76.4%). Dedrick et al. tested three models: an eight-factor model in which the factors correlated, an eight-factor model in which they did not, and a one-factor model. The eight-factor models reflected the eight cross-informant scales.

Among the fit indexes used were the comparative fit index (CFI), the Tucker-Lewis index (TLI), the Bentler-Bonett index (BBI), and the root mean square error of approximation (RMSEA). For the present, we offer only a few simple guidelines for understanding these indexes. A high CFI, TLI, and BBI favor the model being tested, and .90 is a desirable result. A low RMSEA also favors the model being tested. A result below .10 is sometimes viewed as desirable. Some researchers use more exacting standards, such as .08 or .05.

Table 2.4, which presents findings from three studies for comparison, includes those reported by Dedrick et al. (1997). Besides the CFI, TLI, BBI, and RMSEA, the table includes less reliable fit indexes needed for comparison. The eight-factor, uncorrelated model produced a very poor fit. By contrast, the eight-factor, correlated model produced a consistently good fit. The one-factor model also produced a reasonably good fit.

Heubeck (2000) analyzed profiles of 3,000 clinic-referred children and adolescents, using Achenbach's (1991a) eight-factor cross-informant model and a second eight-factor model presented by DeGroot, Koot, and Verhuest (1994). DeGroot et al. had tested and upheld their model with a Dutch sample. Achenbach (1991a) and Dedrick et al. (1997) had conducted comparable studies in the United States, and Achenbach's study had included both models. Heubeck's study took place in Sydney, Australia. Thus, when Heubeck reported on the four sets of findings together, results became available for both models and for all three countries.

Table 2.4 Selected Results for One-Factor, Eight-Factor Uncorrelated, and Eight-Factor Correlated Models of the CBCL

Model	Author	Sample	Fit Indexes[a]			Robust Fit Indexes[b]			
			GFI	AGFI	RMR	CFI	TLI	BBI	RMSEA
One-factor	Dedrick et al. (1997)	U.S.	—	—	—	.85	.85	.83	.104
	Achenbach (1991a)	U.S.	.86	.85	.109	.84	.84	.84	.109
	Heubeck (2000)	Sydney	.83	.82	.121	.80	.80	.80	.122
Achenbach	Dedrick et al. (1997)	U.S.	—	—	—	.33	.32	.33	.220
Uncorrelated[c]	Achenbach (1991a)	U.S.	.43	.41	.217	.34	.33	.34	.222
	Heubeck (2000)	Sydney	.45	.42	.215	.37	.35	.36	.219
Achenbach	Dedrick et al. (1997)	U.S.	.91	.90	.086	.91	.91	.89	.079
Correlated[c]	Achenbach (1991a)	U.S.	.91	.91	.085	.90	.90	.90	.085
	Heubeck (2000)	Sydney	.90	.89	.092	.89	.88	.88	.092
	DeGroot et al. (1994)	Holland	.88	.88	.096	—	—	—	—
DeGroot et al.	Achenbach (1991a)	U.S.	.91	.91	.085	.90	.90	.90	.085
Correlated[c]	Heubeck (2000)	Sydney	.90	.90	.091	.89	.89	.89	.091
	DeGroot et al. (1994)	Holland	.88	.88	.096	—	—	—	—

Source: Heubeck (2000).

Note. GFI = Goodness-of-fit index; AGFI = Adjusted goodness-of-fit index; RMR = Root mean residual; CFI = comparative fit index; TLI = Tucker-Lewis index; BBI = Bentler-Bonett index; RMSEA = root mean square error of approximation.

[a]Highly influenced by sample size.

[b]Not highly influenced by sample size.

[c]An eight-factor model.

All profiles were taken between the years 1983 and 1997. Heubeck (2000) excluded second profiles for any child and records with "too much missing data" (p. 441), leaving 2,237 profiles for analysis. The respondents were 1,523 boys aged 4–17 years and 714 girls aged 4–18 years.

Like Dedrick et al. (1997), Heubeck (2000) used confirmatory factor analysis to analyze the results from Australia. Again, Table 2.4 presents fit indexes. These results were extremely similar to the previous U.S. findings. When the eight cross-informant factors were uncorrelated, Achenbach's (1991a) model again produced very poor results. When these factors were correlated, the results were consistent and greatly improved.

Overall, the model of DeGroot et al. (1994) tested as well as that of Achenbach (1991a)—in fact, marginally better. In Achenbach's (1991a) study, the two models had tested identically; they also consistently showed the slightly lower fit indexes of Dedrick et al. (1997) for Achenbach's model. Thus, the model of DeGroot et al. merits consideration when interpreting CBCL results because it may be slightly better than Achenbach's model.

Practitioners should consider, however, that such comparable results are common with CFA. Scientists sometimes use consistency with theory to decide among multiple models with high fit indexes. We suggest, as an alternative, consistency with results from multiple types of research, perhaps even exploratory factor analysis (EFA) with a separate sample. In the meantime, examiners should give some consideration to any well-supported model of an instrument.

The factor structure of the CBCL, like that of the BASC, appears to be similar across cultures. Thus, measures of this type may be appropriate for studies of multiple cultures (see also Reynolds, Lowe, & Saenz, 1999). Evidence supporting the use of the CBCL with young people of different cultures, except as presented in the manual, is preliminary.

The CBCL and Attention-Deficit/Hyperactivity Disorder

Typically, the CBCL has fared well in assessing ADHD and related difficulties in both referred and nonreferred samples. The test has performed well also in diagnoses of comorbid conditions, such as Oppositional Defiant Disorder (ODD), Conduct Disorder (CD), depressive disorders, and anxiety disorders, when these conditions are measured by structured interviews based on *DSM-III-R* criteria. Zelko (1991) studied the CBCL, the Self-Control Rating Scale, and Conners' Abbreviated Rating Scale. The CBCL was the most effective of the three at discriminating among boys with ADHD, psychiatric controls, and nonpsychiatric controls.

Eiraldi et al. (2000) utilized a sample of 242 children aged 6 years 0 months to 12 years 11 months. The children were referred consecutively; 79% were boys and 76% were White, although the proportion of African Americans,

21%, was also reasonably high. The examinees' IQs, as measured by the Kaufman Brief Intelligence Test, were close to 100. The control group had no psychiatric condition.

In this study, Eiraldi et al. (2000) assessed the sensitivity, specificity, positive predictive power (PPP), and negative predictive power (NPP) of selected scales when used to assess for ADHD. The researchers defined these terms essentially as follows. The *sensitivity* of a scale is the proportion of examinees who have a particular disorder and are correctly classified by the scale as having it. A scale's *specificity* is the proportion of examinees who do not have the disorder and are correctly classified as not having it. Many researchers prefer positive predictive power to sensitivity and negative predictive power to specificity. *Positive predictive power* is the probability that an examinee who has a particular symptom—or a score above a particular cutoff point—has the disorder in question. *Negative predictive power* is the probability that an examinee who does not have such a symptom or score does not have the disorder in question (Rapid Reference 2.6).

≡Rapid Reference 2.6

Definitions

Sensitivity: The proportion of examinees who
(a) have a particular disorder, and
(b) are correctly classified by the scale as having it.

Specificity: The proportion of examinees who
(a) do not have a particular disorder, and
(b) are correctly classified by the scale as not having it.

Positive predictive power: The probability that an examinee who
(a) has a particular symptom, or
(b) has a score above a particular cutoff point
has the disorder in question.

Negative predictive power: The probability that an examinee who
(a) does not have a particular symptom, or
(b) does not have a score above a particular cutoff point
does not have the disorder in question.

Table 2.5 shows most of the results reported by the researchers for the CBCL. For more complete results, including those for the Devereux Scales of Mental Disorders (DSMD), see Eiraldi et al. (2000), especially Tables 4 and 6 in that work. A PPP or NPP of .90 (or a corrected PPP or NPP of .65) is a criterion sometimes used to indicate good discrimination. The PPP and corrected PPP (cPPP) values show that the Attention Problems scale most often correctly identified examinees with ADHD when T scores were high. At T scores of 55, 60, and 65, prediction was very low. The NPP and cNPP columns show that the scale best predicted examinees without ADHD when T scores were low.

Jensen et al. (1996) studied 482 children of military families, examining protocols from the CBCL and the Diagnostic Interview Schedule for Children (DISC 2.1). The children ranged from 5–17 years of age. The sample was then narrowed to children who had one or more of five selected DISC 2.1 diagnoses

Table 2.5 Convergent and Discriminant Validity Indexes for the CBCL when Assessing for ADHD

Cutoff[a]	Convergent Validity Index			Discriminant Validity Index		
	Sensitivity	PPP	cPPP	Specificity	NPP	cNPP
Combined children with ADHD (n = 115) vs. controls (n = 36)						
$T \geq 55$	1.0	.83	.30	.37	1.0	1.0
$T \geq 60$	.99	.85	.37	.44	.94	.92
$T \geq 65$	.76	.89	.53	.69	.48	.32
$T \geq 70$	.50	.91	.61	.83	.34	.14
Children with ADHD, Inattentive Type (n = 58), vs. controls (n = 36)						
$T \geq 55$	1.0	.72	.26	.36	1.0	1.0
$T \geq 60$	1.0	.74	.26	.44	1.0	1.0
$T \geq 65$	.81	.81	.50	.69	.69	.50
$T \geq 70$	.52	.83	.56	.83	.52	.22

Note. PPP = positive predictive power; cPPP = corrected positive predictive power; NPP = negative predictive power; cNPP = corrected negative predictive power.

[a]A T score on the Attention Problems scale.

(Table 2.6), according to either the child's or the parent's responses. Finally, a sample of 201 children was selected so that half were above the 80th percentile and half were below it. All participants were from military families, however, so the results may not be generalizable to the broader population of children in the United States.

The researchers used Pearson's r to compare scores from both tests with external criteria consisting of five components obtained through principal components analysis. Jensen et al. (1996) obtained results for CBCL scores in a first analysis and for derived cutoff scores in a second analysis. The correlations were generally low, perhaps because scaled scores were compared with face-to-face interviews, a very different method (Jensen et al.). One correlation, that between CBCL Hyperactivity scores and the factor Hyperactivity and School Dysfunction/Disability/Use of School Services, was large ($r = .47$, $p \leq .001$; compare $r = .35$, $p \leq .001$ for the DISC 2.1).

The researchers also assessed differences between CBCL correlations and DISC 2.1 correlations with the five components. The few statistically significant differences found—3 (10%) for standard scores and 0 (0%) for cut scores—may have been due to chance. Finally, the DISC 2.1 showed a higher percentage of correct classifications than the CBCL (83% vs. 74%).

Jensen et al. (1996) also compared the CBCL and DISC 2.1 with scores on

Table 2.6 Diagnoses of Respondents in Investigation of the CBCL and DISC

Disorder	Percent of Total Sample
Any anxiety disorder	30.0
Depression/Psychasthenia	7.0
ADHD	30.1
ODD	7.5
CD	3.0
Combined	77.6

Source: Jensen et al. (1996).

Note. ADHD = Attention-Deficit/Hyperactivity Disorder, ODD = Oppositional Defiant Disorder, CD = Conduct Disorder.

the Child Depression Inventory (CDI) and the Revised Children's Manifest Anxiety Scale (RCMAS). Correlations with the CBCL were relatively large but potentially inflated because the CDI and RCMAS apparently were treated as one variable. To summarize, this study provided little support for the CBCL as opposed to the DISC 2.1. We note, however, that dimensional measures such as the CBCL and categorical systems such as the *DSM-IV* are very different. The results of comparisons of this type are at best difficult to interpret.

THE CRS-R

Practical Merits of the CRS-R

The CRS-R inventories are unique among major checklists in their focus on attention disorders and related symptoms. Most scales, such as Anxious/Shy, have an established relationship to ADHD and related conditions. Each version of the CRS-R contains an overall pathology measure called Conners' Global Index (CGI), but this distinctive index is a convenient, 10-item measure of relatively general symptoms rather than an omnibus scale. Thus, the CRS-R may be most appropriate when an examinee has, or is suspected of having an attention-related condition.

The CRS-R has a single manual for all versions. The manual is well-written and thorough in its coverage of major aspects of testing. Practitioners are likely to understand most of it, except for the statistical portions, which may be difficult. The CRS-R manual provides an informative series of case studies, with indications for *DSM-IV* diagnosis, interpretation, further examination, and the like. Finally, the manual describes in detail the qualifications needed to administer the inventory.

The instructions are brief and clear for parents and teachers. Very similar instructions to the Self-Report Scale, however, may be difficult for some adolescents. Here, less brevity for the sake of clarity probably would have been an asset. In addition, the tone of the instructions is somewhat formal for adolescents.

CRS-R items present four response options, as the BASC does, rather than three, as the CBCL does. The additional choice may enhance the comfort level of adolescent respondents. The four options may slightly increase the difficulty, particularly because each response option has more than one possible meaning (e.g., a score denoting *very much true* can also mean *very often, very frequent;* one denoting *pretty much true* can mean *often, quite a bit*).

Among the useful features of the CRS-R inventories are carbonless forms. In addition, the CRS-R has long and short forms, with the former providing a more extensive profile, and the latter, brief administration and a convenient, small size. Practitioners can easily score the three composites of the CRS-R while scoring the scales themselves. Finally, the CRS-R provides *DSM-IV* Inattentive and Hyperactive-Impulsive scales, together with a third ADHD index.

The CPRS-R:L (Conners' Parent Rating Scales–Revised:Long Version) is accompanied by a 4-page Parent Feedback Form (PFF), which explains in simple terms the uses and reasons for testing and other ethical concerns. The PFF also identifies services and information that parents can expect to receive from the examiner. This form is easy to produce and provides important information that all parents of clients should have. This information is equally relevant to other personality tests and clinicians should provide it, perhaps in conjunction with a form similar to the PFF.

The CRS-R, unlike the revisions of many other rating scales, incorporates content not driven solely by items contained in earlier versions of the same scale. As a result, the scale is fairly reflective of current thought on childhood emotional and behavioral problems. Conversely, the test retains some of its best-supported content, such as Conners' Global Index. The scale construction procedure has led to fairly similar items within each scale, making interpretation easier. Finally, the parent and teacher versions of the scales correspond well, facilitating comparisons in a multi-informant assessment.

Despite these advantages, the CRS-R has some notable limitations. The scales assess for oppositional forms of conduct problems but omit more serious difficulties such as stealing, lying, and vandalism. Coverage of depression is minimal. For several CRS-R subscales, more research is needed to support some aspects of validity. Most notably, little evidence is available for the validity of the subscales with preschool children, although the norming sample includes children as young as 3 years. Evidence from past versions is unlikely to be applicable to the new scales because the content is extensively revised.

Finally, relatively little is done with the distinction between internalizing and externalizing items of the CRS-R. This is curious because the two concepts are relevant to attention disorders and related conditions. This distinction figures prominently—and usefully—in the Achenbach scales and particularly in the

BASC. The CRS-R does not provide a thorough assessment of internalizing problems in themselves (Kamphaus & Frick, 2002).

Technical Merits of the CRS-R

The most important technical advance of the CRS-R is its norming samples. For the six versions of the revised Conners scales, norming samples ranged in size from 1,897 to 3,486 examinees and were representative of most of North America. Separate norms are available for boys and girls, and at 3-year age intervals. The sample for the CTRS-R (Conners' Teacher Rating Scales–Revised), for example, consisted of 1,973 children and adolescents, 965 male and 1,008 female, from 45 states and 10 provinces throughout the United States and Canada. Combined gender norms, however, are not provided. All children and adolescents in the norming samples attended regular classes.

Table 2.7 shows percentages represented by ethnic groups as reported by parents, teachers, and adolescents completing the long versions of CRS-R. As self-reported by parents, Whites were overrepresented, whereas African Americans and Hispanics were underrepresented. The percentages provided by teachers were about the same, but slightly more representative of North American ethnicities (Conners, 1997). Adolescents who provided ratings differed in

Table 2.7 Self-Identified Ethnicity of Parents Completing the CRS-R[a,b]

	Percentage[a]		
Ethnic Group	Parent	Teacher	Adolescent
Caucasian/White	83[b]	78[b]	62[b]
African American/Black	4.8	10.2	29.9
Hispanic	3.5	5.8	2.3
Asian American	2.2	1.6	1.6
Native American	1.1	1.5	1.3
Other[c]	4.9	2.8	3.1

[a]Version R:L.

[b]As reported in manual (Conners, 1997).

[c]Also includes No Ethnic Information Provided.

average age from children and adolescents rated only by parents and teachers. This difference may explain why adolescents' self-reports of ethnicity diverged markedly from parents' and teachers' reports. Another possibility is that the adolescent self-report version produced a low response rate on this item. If so, ethnic figures for the parent and teacher forms are more reliable. Research is necessary to arrive at an explanation for the discrepant self-report figures.

For participating parents, the median annual income range was $40,001–50,000. This figure is above the national median but at least is provided. Respondents' incomes and other SES variables are difficult to collect; many test manuals omit them entirely.

Reliabilities of the CRS-R were generally good ($\alpha \geq .80$) and frequently very good ($\alpha \geq .90$). The exceptions were rare. On the CPRS-R:L, results were somewhat lower for the CGI (Conners' Global Index) Emotional Lability scale ($\alpha = .667–.795$ for males, $.715–.74$ for females) and the Psychosomatic scale ($\alpha = .693–.832$ for males, $.748–.807$ for females). On the CPRS-R:S, the Hyperactivity scale produced somewhat lower reliabilities for 15–17 year olds ($\alpha = .693$ for males, $.685$ for females). On the CTRS, the CGI Emotional Lability scale was improved, though still somewhat low in the 15–17 year range for males ($\alpha = .667$) and particularly females ($\alpha = .545$; Conners, 1997).

Test-retest reliabilities are available for a 6–8 week interval between testings. Table 2.8 shows reliability ranges. As the table indicates, results were variable

Table 2.8 Test-Retest Reliability Coefficients for the CRS-R

Version	Low	Scale	High	Scale
CPRS-R:L	.47	Anxious/Shy	.85	Hyperactivity
CTRS-R:L	.47	Cognitive Problems/Inattention *DSM-IV* Hyperactivity/ Impulsivity	.88	Anxious/Shy
CASS:L	.73	Cognitive Problems/Inattention	.89	Emotional Problems
CPRS-R:S	.62	Oppositional	.85	Hyperactivity
CTRS-R:S	.72	Hyperactivity	.92	Cognitive Problems/ Inattention
CASS:S	.72	Conduct Problems	.87	ADHD Index

Note. Low = Lowest reliability; High = Highest reliability.

for the CPRS-R:L and the CTRS-R:L but generally good for CASS:L and for the short forms.

The statistical development of the scales was thorough. Principle axis factoring (PAF) was among the exploratory techniques used, and results were generally good (e.g., Conners, Sitarenios, Parker, & Epstein, 1998). Similarly, CFA results were good for all versions, including the new adolescent self-report (Table 2.9).

Some of the language used in the CRS-R manual (Conners, 1997) should be more exact; at times, simple numbers should replace existing verbal descriptions. The manual reports that the majority of site coordinators were school psychologists. A percentage, such as 95% or 53%, would be more informative.

The manual (Conners, 1997) also reports that some group administration was used with the self-report forms. Group administration would affect the results obtained with the norming sample and therefore would affect the validity and reliability of the standardized results of clinicians' evaluations. The extent of this effect would depend in part on how much group administration occurred. The effect should be investigated and, if it is large, group and individual norms should be provided.

In addition, reporting should be made understandable to nonstatisticians. The section on Age and Sex Effects in Chapter 7 of the manual (Conners, 1997), for example, presents ANOVA results with little further comment. Even clinicians with considerable experience could have trouble deciphering these statistics. ANOVA in particular is intimidating and hard to understand

Table 2.9 Goodness-of-Fit Indexes for the CRS-R

Version	Index		
	GFI[a]	Adjusted GFI[a]	RMS[b]
CPRS-R:S	.936	.928	.042
CTRS-R:S	.907	.877	.062
CASS:S	.932	.912	.048

Note. GFI = Goodness-of-fit index; RMS = Root mean square residual.

[a]Not highly influenced by sample size.

[b]Highly influenced by sample size.

for most people who have encountered it. These findings should be clarified and interpreted for practitioners.

Another reporting issue is effect size, as defined previously in this chapter. Any reporting should include information on how much of a relationship was found, in addition to whether the relationship may be generalized to the population. In the section noted above, the only effect sizes reported were F values. These statistics are poor estimates of effect size because they are highly sensitive to sample size. A more informative measure would be Pearson's r.

A final reporting issue is summarization. Summaries in the CRS-R manual (Conners, 1997) sometimes omitted limitations that were evident in the results themselves (e.g., compare the summary on p. 119 with the results on p. 118).

Like the CBCL, the CRS-R has a long history of research. The usefulness of this research is attenuated by the fact that much of it addressed earlier versions of the scales, such as the CTRS-39 (teachers' version, 39 items) and CPRS-48 (parents' version, 48 items). Wainwright (1996) has summarized many of the available studies in an Annotated Bibliography covering 451 studies and 25 years of investigation. Results come from such diverse countries as China, Brazil, Germany, and Australia.

Conners (Wainwright, 1996) describes these studies as examinations of the CRS. This may be true, but it is not always clear from the entries. Some of the studies, such as De Jong and Das-Smaal (1990; cited in Wainwright, 1996) appear able to provide only limited data on the CRS. De Jong and Das-Smaal found an association between the Star Counting Test (SCT) and two dissimilar CRS scales. Although sound as an indication of discriminant validity, the association was modest, perhaps because of limitations with the SCT, the CRS, or both. This finding may say more about the lesser-known SCT than about the better-established CRS, with its long history of research.

Conversely, excellent results reported by Glow and Glow (1980; cited in Wainwright, 1996) depend on the construct validity of a test under development that was being compared with the CRS. Finally, some of the studies (e.g., Pless, Taylor, & Arsenault, 1995; Rickard & Woodes-de-Rael, 1987; both cited in Wainwright) apparently were meant to address the characteristics measured by the CRS rather than the scales themselves.

Most studies in Wainwright's (1996) bibliography, however, are appropriate for the stated subject. The summaries are apt and useful. Moreover, the re-

CAUTION

The BASC, the CBCL, and the CRS-R appear simple to use and interpret, but this appearance is deceptive. Extensive graduate-level training in individual assessment, childhood psychopathology, and psychometrics is critical to the choice, application, and interpretation of any of these scales. Diagnosis and treatment planning requires a skilled clinician, not simply a technician.

search itself provides copious information on the utility and on the statistical properties of the Conners inventories.

CONCLUDING COMMENT

All of the scales discussed here have reasonably sound psychometric properties, although the BASC and CBCL have advantages over the CRS-R on the whole. Non-English-language versions of the scales vary in their quality and applicability and require careful inspection by an examiner fluent in the target language prior to the decision to use them. All three scales are easy to administer but are *Category C* tests with regard to their use in diagnosis and their clinical interpretation. Thus, extensive graduate-level training in individual assessment, childhood psychopathology, and psychometrics are prerequisites to choice, application, and interpretation of these scales.

🐟 TEST YOURSELF 🐟

1. **Reliability can take the form of consistency from one _____ to another.**
    (a) group
    (b) time period
    (c) region
    (d) group, time period, or region

2. **Validity is the accuracy of**
    (a) a test.
    (b) performance on a test.
    (c) interpretations of test performance.
    (d) responses to test items.

3. **Research on the BASC, the CBCL, and the CRS-R has shown that their reliability and validity**

   (a) are generally sound, supported by a considerable amount of available research.

   (b) are firmly established, so that little or no further research is needed.

   (c) are dubious, with promising results from previous years now discredited.

   (d) are difficult to establish because psychological characteristics are inherently unmeasurable.

4. **A norming sample allows practitioners to compare their examinees' scores with**

   (a) scores of others of their own age group.

   (b) an ideal score representing perfect performance.

   (c) an empirical cutoff representing ineffective performance.

   (d) the performance of clearly superior individuals.

5. **The major advantage of the BASC is its norming sample, which**

   (a) is much larger than those of other rating scales, allowing comparisons with smaller groups.

   (b) is so large that few studies of the test's reliability and validity are necessary.

   (c) includes diverse ethnic groups for the first time in rating scale development.

   (d) eliminates the outdated practice of providing separate male and female norms.

6. **A second advantage of the BASC is its composites, which measure**

   (a) highly specific constructs, such as Hyperactivity and Social Phobia.

   (b) only directly observable behavior, as opposed to Aggression and other theoretical traits.

   (c) conceptually interesting Freudian constructs, such as the Oedipus and Electra complexes.

   (d) strongly supported Internalizing and Externalizing constructs, along with a cutting-edge Adaptive Skills construct.

7. **A practical advantage of the CBCL is**

   (a) extensive administration guidelines found in the manual.

   (b) *T* scores requiring no calculations.

   (c) brief, simple scoring procedures.

   (d) high reliability over a one-year period.

(continued)

8. A major development that emerged with the 1991 revisions of the CBCL was

(a) *cross-population profiles,* score patterns that are consistent from one protocol and age-sex combination to another.

(b) *cross-informant syndromes,* sets of items that are consistent from one protocol and age-sex combination to another.

(c) *cross-factor matrices,* correlations with the factors being measured that are consistent from one factor to another.

(d) *cross-country skewing,* a pattern of nonnormality that closely matches results from most regions of the U.S. and Canada.

9. The CRS-R inventories have

(a) a single manual that is well-written and clear throughout.

(b) a single manual that is well-written and clear, except for statistical portions.

(c) six detailed, well-written manuals with copious supportive materials.

(d) six highly technical manuals that require substantial expertise to understand.

10. The most important technical advance of the CRS-R is its

(a) consistency from one administration to another.

(b) multistage item development process.

(c) factor-analytic results.

(d) norming samples.

Answers: 1. d; 2. c; 3. a; 4. a; 5. a; 6. d; 7. b; 8. b; 9. b; 10. d

Three

THE BEHAVIOR ASSESSMENT SYSTEM FOR CHILDREN

We first present the Behavior Assessment System for Children (BASC), the newest of the major rating scale inventories. The three main components of the BASC are the Teacher Rating Scales (TRS), the Parent Rating Scales (PRS), and the Self-Report of Personality (SRP). The TRS and PRS are appropriate for ages 2 years 6 months 0 days through 18 years 11 months 30 days. The SRP is appropriate for ages 8 years 0 months 0 days through 18 years 11 months 30 days. As noted in Chapter 2, readability statistics have been calculated for the BASC PRS and for the child and adolescent versions of the SRP. The results are extremely good, showing readability grade levels of 2.0, 2.0, and 3.0, respectively. Rapid References 3.1 and 3.2 outline publication information about the BASC and the BASC Monitor for ADHD Rating Scales.

The TRS and PRS are quantitative rating scales providing a stem to which the respondent replies *Never, Sometimes, Often,* or *Almost Always.* The TRS provides a comprehensive review of behavior at school, and the PRS provides similar information for the home and community settings. Table 3.1 lists the TRS and PRS scales and their respective age ranges. Table 3.2 provides definitions of the scales.

The SRP is an omnibus personality inventory that presents statements to which a child or adolescent respondent replies *true* or *false.* This inventory surveys both personality and clinical dimensions of behavior. Table 3.3 lists the scales of the SRP and the age range of each version. Table 3.4 provides scale definitions.

≡ *Rapid Reference 3.1*

Behavior Assessment for Children (BASC)

Authors: Cecil R. Reynolds & R. W. Kamphaus

Publication Date: 1998

What the test measures: Behavior problems, adaptive behaviors, and self-report of thoughts, emotions, self-perception; history form included.

Administration time: Rating scales, 15 min
Self-report, 20 min
Direct observation scale, 15 min

Qualification of examiners: Graduate- or professional-level training in psychological assessment.

Publisher: American Guidance Service
4201 Woodland Road
Circle Pines, MN 55014-1796
800-328-2560
www.agsnet.com

Prices: Starter set: $89.95 (as of September, 2001)

≡ *Rapid Reference 3.2*

BASC Monitor for ADHD Rating Scales

Authors: R. W. Kamphaus & Cecil R. Reynolds

Publication Date: 1998

What the test measures: Attention problems, hyperactivity, internalizing problems, adaptive skills.

Administration time: 5–10 min

Qualification of examiners: Graduate- or professional-level training in psychological assessment.

Publisher: American Guidance Service
4201 Woodland Road
Circle Pines, MN 55014-1796
800-328-2560
www.agsnet.com

Prices: Starter set: Hand-score version, $104.95
Computer-score version, $209.95
Licensing available
(all as of September, 2001)

Table 3.1 Composites and Scales of the TRS and PRS

Composite/Scale	Teacher Rating Scales			Parent Rating Scales		
	Preschool, 2.5–5	Child, 6–11	Adolescent, 12–18	Preschool, 2.5–5	Child, 6–11	Adolescent, 12–18
Externalizing Problems	*	*	*	*	*	*
Aggression	*	*	*	*	*	*
Hyperactivity	*	*	*	*	*	*
Conduct Problems		*	*		*	*
Internalizing Problems	*	*	*	*	*	*
Anxiety	*	*	*	*	*	*
Depression	*	*	*	*	*	*
Somatization	*	*	*	*	*	*
School Problems		*	*			
Attention Problems	*	*	*	*	*	*
Learning Problems		*	*			
Other Problems						
Atypicality	*	*	*	*	*	*
Withdrawal	*	*	*	*	*	*
Adaptive Skills	*	*	*	*	*	*
Adaptability	*	*		*	*	
Leadership		*	*	*	*	*
Social Skills	*	*	*	*	*	*
Study Skills		*	*			
Behavioral Symptoms Index	*	*	*	*	*	*

Note. Italicized scales compose the Behavioral Symptoms Index.

Table 3.2 TRS and PRS Scale Definitions

Scale	Definition
Adaptability	The ability to adapt readily to changes in the environment
Anxiety	The tendency to be nervous, fearful, or worried about real or imagined problems
Aggression	The tendency to act in a hostile manner (either verbal or physical) that is threatening to others
Attention Problems	The tendency to be easily distracted and unable to concentrate more than momentarily
Atypicality	The tendency to behave in ways that are immature, considered odd, or commonly associated with psychosis (such as experiencing visual or auditory hallucinations)
Conduct Problems	The tendency to engage in antisocial and rule-breaking behavior, including destruction of property
Depression	Feelings of unhappiness, sadness, and stress that may result in an inability to carry out everyday activities (neurovegetative symptoms) or that may bring on thoughts of suicide
Hyperactivity	The tendency to be overly active, rush through work or activities, and act without thinking
Leadership	The skills associated with accomplishing academic, social, or community goals, including in particular the ability to work well with others
Learning Problems	The presence of academic difficulties, particularly in understanding or completing schoolwork
Social Skills	The skills necessary for interacting successfully with peers and adults in home, school, and community settings
Somatization	The tendency to be overly sensitive to and complain about relatively minor physical problems and discomforts
Study Skills	The skills that are conducive to strong academic performance, including organizational skills and good study habits
Withdrawal	The tendency to evade others to avoid social contact

Note. Italicized scales compose the Behavioral Symptoms Index.

Table 3.3 Composites and Scales in the SRP

Composite/Scale	Child, 8–11	Adolescent, 12–18
Clinical Maladjustment	*	*
Anxiety	*	*
Atypicality	*	*
Locus of Control	*	*
Social Stress	*	*
Somatization		*
School Maladjustment	*	*
Attitude to School	*	*
Attitude to Teachers	*	*
Sensation Seeking		*
Other Problems		
Depression	*	*
Sense of Inadequacy	*	*
Personal Adjustment	*	*
Relations with Parents	*	*
Interpersonal Relations	*	*
Self-Esteem	*	*
Self Reliance	*	*
Emotional Symptoms Index	*	*

Note. Italicized scales compose the Emotional Symptoms Index.

Table 3.4 SRP Scale Definitions

Scale	Definition
Anxiety	Feelings of nervousness, worry, and fear; the tendency to be overwhelmed by problems
Attitude to School	Feelings of alienation, hostility, and dissatisfaction regarding school
Attitude to Teachers	Feelings of resentment for and dislike of teachers; beliefs that teachers are unfair, uncaring, or overly demanding
Atypicality	The tendency toward severe mood swings, bizarre thoughts, subjective experiences, or obsessive-compulsive thoughts and behaviors often considered odd
Depression	Feelings of unhappiness, sadness, and dejection; a belief that nothing goes right
Interpersonal Relations	The perception of having good social relationships and friendships with peers
Locus of Control	The belief that rewards and punishments are controlled by external events or other people
Relations with Parents	A positive regard toward parents and a feeling of being esteemed by them
Self-Esteem	Feelings of self-esteem, self-respect, and self-acceptance
Self-Reliance	Confidence in one's ability to solve problems; a belief in one's personal dependability and decisiveness
Sensation Seeking	The tendency to take risks, to like noise, and to seek excitement
Sense of Inadequacy	Perceptions of being unsuccessful in school, unable to achieve one's goals, and generally inadequate
Social Stress	Feelings of stress and tension in personal relationships; a feeling of being excluded from social activities
Somatization	The tendency to be overly sensitive to, experience, or complain about relatively minor physical problems and discomforts

Note. Italicized scales compose the Emotional Symptoms Index.

ADMINISTRATION AND SCORING

The computer-scored and hand-scored record forms of the BASC present response options next to the respective items, rather than on a separate sheet. This approach reduces error and limits difficulty. Test difficulty can interfere with a respondent's attention and willingness to complete a test, particularly for a child.

DON'T FORGET

Although each BASC record form can be hand-scored in 10–20 minutes, computer scoring is encouraged and takes only about 2 minutes per protocol. Computer scoring provides additional information that cannot be obtained through hand scoring.

For the hand-scored versions, responses transfer directly to a scoring sheet concealed beneath the record form. This expedient eliminates errors in transcription. The items are reordered on the form so that the child, parent, or teacher may not deduce correspondences between the items and subtests and subsequently make invalid responses. Later, the scoring sheet allows examiners to sum the responses easily by viewing a simple pattern of lines and arrows.

The BASC's ease of responding does not eliminate the need for rapport. Examiners should administer the BASC with as much care as any other instrument. Respondents should feel relaxed and comfortable with the test and setting, just as with lengthier standardized tests. With any test, a respondent may linger over the items, lose interest in completing the test form, or respond so as to create a good or bad impression. Good rapport can help to reduce such difficulties. Young children require particular attention; they can react unexpectedly to testing (Reynolds & Kamphaus, 1998; Sattler, 1992).

Preparation

All Forms

Examiners can administer the BASC with little additional material. A pen or pencil and a hard surface such as a desk are sufficient. A clipboard is acceptable if no desk or table is available. Markers and felt-tip pens are not advisable for the hand-scored protocols because responses must penetrate to the self-scoring sheet beneath the response form (Reynolds & Kamphaus, 1998).

The Parent Rating Scales

The BASC PRS takes about 10 to 20 minutes to complete. The cover of the form presents instructions, and the top of the next page provides space for information about the child or adolescent. If possible, the parent should complete this form in a controlled setting such as an examiner's office. The PRS is important to diagnosis and treatment planning, so an uncontrolled setting is generally preferable if the alternative is to obtain an uncompleted form. In addition, the form may be mailed if a parent does not reside locally. An audiotape is available for parents with reading problems. The PRS forms are also available in Spanish.

The Teacher Rating Scales

Any adult who has had an extended opportunity to observe the child or adolescent in a school, preschool, or similar setting may complete the TRS. A teacher, a teacher's aide, a daycare worker, or another adult in a similar role is an appropriate respondent. For school-age examinees, a teacher working in a fairly organized classroom setting is best. The respondent should have had considerable contact with the young person. Contact of several days a week for two to eight weeks should be sufficient. In addition, multiple ratings from teachers of different classrooms can help to show how a young person responds to varied teaching styles, academic demands, and disciplinary standards (Reynolds & Kamphaus, 1998).

The TRS takes about 10 to 20 minutes to complete. The cover of the form presents instructions, and the top of the next page provides space for information about both the young person (to be filled out by the examiner) and the adult respondent (to be filled out by the respondent). If possible, the respondent should complete this form in a single sitting free from distractions. Information about the type of class (such as special education) may also be important. Respondents' perceptions may differ depending on the type of class.

Rapport

The Self-Report of Personality Protocol

The age range of the BASC SRP extends downward to 8 years, and very young respondents can present special challenges. Examiners should present the BASC to young children in an engaging manner and should neither intimidate nor distract them. Praise should be generous but should never be repetitious and predictable, causing an examinee to become skeptical or accustomed to it.

Some older children also may resist testing and therefore require supervision. Left to themselves, they may respond at random or refuse to complete the inventory. Finally, rapport with children in detention facilities and other forensic settings may require special approaches. Any difficulties should be addressed as they would in those settings with other tests (Reynolds & Kamphaus, 1998).

The Parent and Teacher Rating Scales
Adherence to high professional standards enhances rapport with adult respondents. Professionalism is important to allay any fears the respondent may have about the use of the information obtained. Parents in particular may be concerned about the effect this information may have on their children. In addition, examiners should be honest about the intended use of the results and about similar concerns, such as the reasons for the evaluation, the limits of confidentiality, and applicable local laws.

Instructions and Reinforcement

The Self-Report of Personality Protocol
The instructions should be understandable for most respondents. Very young children may need additional coaching, especially with the first few items. An examiner might precede an item with, "Listen to this." After reading the item, the examiner might continue, "Are you like that? Or are you not like that?" followed by encouragement to circle the applicable response. An audiotape version is available for children with reading problems.

Examiners should avoid establishing response sets, accidentally leading children to give a single response repeatedly or to present themselves in a positive or negative manner. Positive and negative responses to the items should elicit equivalent praise or reinforcement. If a child endorses the item *Nobody likes me,* a tone of concern is quite natural but can render subsequent results inaccurate. Beginning examiners in particular should exercise caution here.

The Parent Report Form
The instructions to parents suggested in the BASC manual portray parents as experts regarding their children. Thus, the examiner approaches the respondent largely as an equal. The instructions are presented here in a slightly modified form (adapted from Reynolds & Kamphaus, 1998):

You as a parent have observed Larry's behavior a great deal. To evaluate the difficulties he has encountered, I need your help in many ways. One way is to have information about Larry's behavior as you see it. Please read the instructions on this form and respond to all the items, even if some are difficult to answer or do not seem to apply. If you have any questions or would like me to clarify anything, please don't hesitate to ask for my help.

The Teacher Report Form

The instructions to teachers and similar respondents should appeal to their professionalism. Examiners should present themselves primarily as equal partners, rather than as experts providing direction or information. Thus, the suggested instructions provided in the manual portray the examiner as a colleague asking for assistance. For convenience, they are reproduced here (Reynolds & Kamphaus, 1998):

I am evaluating Suzanne and would appreciate your assistance. I would like to know how Suzanne behaves in your class. This form takes 10 to 20 minutes to complete. It would help both Suzanne and me if you would complete it. Please read the instructions on the form and respond to all the items. Call me if you have any questions. I appreciate your help.

Reviewing the Completed BASC Form

All Forms

After administration, scan the completed form for any missing, multiple, or ambiguous responses. Ask the respondent to fill them in or clarify them. If this is not feasible or if the respondent refuses to answer certain items, proceed with scoring. Do not score scales with three or more blank items or composites that include these scales (Reynolds & Kamphaus, 1998).

SCORING

The Self-Report of Personality

Like other BASC protocols, the SRP is unusually easy to hand score. First, tear off the top edge at the perforations. Pull the upper sheet down, separating the

SRP from the Item Scoring Page beneath it. For each item, a 1 or a 0 should be circled. A *true* response becomes a 1 for most but not all items. You will also find a Summary Table and Clinical and Adaptive Profiles on the reverse side of the SRP.

Validity Scales

The BASC adolescent SRP (SRP-A) provides three validity scales, and the child SRP (SRP-C) provides two. Items on such scales appear realistic to respondents, but certain responses or combinations of responses are improbable. The F index is a so-called *fake bad* scale. It represents an unrealistic number of negative responses. Score this index first.

To do so, simply count the number of shaded responses on the Item Scoring Page. Then, circle the corresponding score to the left of the Clinical Profile. If this raw score falls into the region labeled *caution* or *extreme caution,* consider whether the respondent is more likely to have severe difficulties or to have responded misleadingly (Reynolds & Kamphaus, 1998). Your interpretation of SRP and other BASC results will differ accordingly. The F index can be interpreted using the T scores in the Clinical Profile.

The adolescent SRP provides an L index, a so-called *fake good* scale representing an unrealistic number of positive responses. Score this index next, in the far right column of the Item Scoring Page. The L index differs from the F index in that any omitted or double-marked L items should be excluded from scoring (Reynolds & Kamphaus, 1998).

After scoring, circle the appropriate raw score in the L column, just to the right of the F column. If the raw L score falls into the region labeled *caution* or *extreme caution,* consider how consistent the responses are with other information, such as teacher or parent ratings. Inconsistency suggests that an adolescent's responses may be misleadingly positive. As with the F index, your interpretation of SRP and BASC results will vary according to your interpretation of the L score. In addition, the L score can be interpreted using the adjacent T scores.

Both SRP forms include a V index, designed to identify responses that are bizarre because of difficulties with reading comprehension,

DON'T FORGET

T scores and confidence intervals may be graphed to provide a clear visual display of the examinee's profile.

lack of contact with reality, or failure to follow directions. On the Item Scoring Page, these items show only one box, which contains a 1 for a response of *true*. If 1 is circled, count it toward the *V* index score. Ignore any other marks. Record the *V* score in the box above the Summary Table. If this score is 2 or greater, examine the items endorsed. A discussion with the child or adolescent may reveal a reason for these responses.

Clinical and Adaptive Scales

Summing item scores. To score the Clinical Scales of the SRP, add the circled numbers in each horizontal row of the Item Scoring Page. Proceed in the direction of the arrows. Write the sum in the empty box to which the arrows lead. If a row contains more than one empty box, each box will have arrows leading to it. Again, follow the arrows to obtain the correct sum. Some items in a row may be unscorable or omitted. If so, record the number of these items in the diamonds within the empty boxes. This is the number of *omits*.

Several items are not connected to an empty box. They are the *critical items* of the SRP. On the Item Scoring Page, each critical item has a solid box containing the item number. Examiners do not need to score these items but should interpret them separately. They may be disregarded until later.

Each box falls in a shaded or unshaded vertical column. After adding the boxes in each row, do the same for each column. Enter the column sum in the box at the bottom of the column. Each of these sums is the scale score for a subtest. Next, add the diamonds in each column to obtain the number of omits. Enter this number in the diamond at the bottom of the page. If the number of omits is 3 or greater for any column, draw a large X through the corresponding scale score. Exclude that scale score from all of the subsequent steps.

Calculating raw scores. Next, transfer each scale score from the bottom of the Item Scoring Page to the Summary Table. Write the scale score in the column labeled *Sum*. Transfer the number of omits to the column labeled *Omits*.

You can now calculate the raw scores using the formula shown here and in the Summary Table:

$$\underline{\qquad} + (\lozenge \times .5) = \underline{\qquad}.$$

C A U T I O N

Double-check your addition after totaling the item scores.

First, multiply the number of omits ($\lozenge$) by the number shown, .5 in this example. Then add the scale score to the result. Enter the total in the *Raw Score* column, rounding down where necessary.

Locating normative scores. To obtain normative or standard scores, first select one or two norm sets from these four options: *General, Male, Female,* and *Clinical.* Check the corresponding box(es) just above the Summary Table to record your selection(s). Examiners should make this decision before obtaining standard scores. The General and Clinical Norms are often useful. At times, the General and same-sex norms are appropriate (Reynolds & Kamphaus, 1998). See Rapid References 3.3 and 3.4 for additional information.

CAUTION

Never sum raw scores. Wait and sum the standard scores, which often take the form of *T* scores.

DON'T FORGET

Do not calculate raw or standard scores for any scale that has three or more omits.

Find the appropriate table by locating the section for the SRP-C or the SRP-A. Next, locate the desired norm group: *General, Male, Female,* or *Clinical.* Finally, locate the table for the examinee's specific age group, such as *Ages 12–14.* Some sections are not subdivided into specific age groups.

After finding the correct norm table, follow the steps shown in Rapid Reference 3.5. When you have located a normative score, you can construct a 90% confidence interval around it using the whole number at the bottom of the column. Subtract this number from the raw score to produce the lower limit of the confidence interval. Add the number to the raw score to produce the upper limit. Record these limits in the Summary Table under *90% Conf. Interval.*

Scoring the Composites and the Emotional Symptoms Index. The Summary Table contains three sections labeled *School Maladjustment Composite, Clinical Maladjustment Composite,* and *Personal Adjustment Composite.* In each section, add the *T* scores and enter the result in the box directly below them. You may then convert this sum to an additional *T* score using the tables in Appendix A just after the normative score tables. To use the *T* score tables, find the Sum of *T* scores in the central columns, then follow it out to a *T* score column at the far left or right of the table. Place this *T* score, if desired, in the rounded box below the sum of *T* scores in the Summary Table.

To calculate the *T* score for the Emotional Symptoms Index (ESI), first fill

≡Rapid Reference 3.3

Characteristics of the Four Sets of BASC Norms

General Norms

- Indicate a child's standing when compared with the general population
- Are based on a large national sample that is representative of the population regarding sex, ethnicity, and clinical or special education classification; for the PRS, parent education also included
- Produce scores subdivided by age; comparisons with children of the same age as the examinee
- Show sex differences on subtests such as Aggression and Depression
- Are helpful in diagnosing needs for special services
- Are used when diagnosing conditions more common for one sex than for another
- Are recommended for general use

Male and Female Norms

- Are based on subsets within the general sample
- Produce scores subdivided by both age and sex; comparisons with children of the same age and sex as the examinee
- Do not show sex differences in examinees' scores on such tests as Aggression and Depression
- Aid in clinical diagnosis of examinees who depart from behavior typical of their own sex

Clinical Norms

- Are based on smaller samples
- Are most helpful when an examinee's difficulties are relatively extreme
- Can produce an interpretable pattern of scores when the General Norms show only a high, flat profile
- Can show an overall level of difficulty when difficulties are extreme, but can best identify specific problems such as ADHD or social maladjustment

in the ovals in the ESI column. To do so, simply transfer the numbers from the corresponding T scores to the left of the ovals. Where indicated, however, you must subtract the T scores from 100 and enter the difference. Add the ovals and enter the sum in the rectangle labeled *Emotional Symptoms Index*. Finally, find the T score for this sum using the same section as for the composites, above. Construction of confidence intervals for the composites and the ESI is the same as for scale scores, except that the whole number used is from the composite and ESI tables.

≡*Rapid Reference 3.4*

SRP Scales That Tend to Show Sex Differences in Raw Scores

Higher Scores for Females
- Anxiety
- Interpersonal Relations

Higher Scores for Males
- Sensation Seeking
- Attitude to School
- Attitude to Teachers
- Self-Esteem

≡*Rapid Reference 3.5*

Four Steps to Find and Record a BASC Normative Score

Step 1. In the norm table, find the raw score in the far left or right column.

Step 2. Follow the row across to the column for the scale being scored, such as Attitude to School.

Step 3. In this column, find the normative score, labeled *T*, and the percentile rank, labeled *%ile*.

Step 4. Enter these numbers in the Summary Table in the columns headed *T score* and *%ile Rank*.

Example. Amanda is 9 years old, so you have examined her using the SRP-C. She has been referred for special services. Her difficulties are moderate to mild; therefore, you use the General Norms. Her raw score for Attitude to School is 5. You find the SRP-C section in Appendix A and locate the *General* table. After finding the raw score 5, you read across to the column headed *Attitude to School*. For Amanda's raw score, the *T* score is 57 and the percentile rank is 73. You enter these numbers in the Summary Table.

Score Comparisons

Identifying High and Low Scale T Scores. For any composite and for the ESI, the examiner may identify which scale scores are significantly different from their respective means. The *T* scores for the Attitude to School, Attitude to Teachers, and Sensation Seeking scales, for example, may each be compared to the mean *T* score of the School Maladjustment Composite. To make these comparisons, first calculate the composite or ESI mean by dividing the sum of *T* scores by the number of *T* scores. For the School Maladjustment Composite, divide by 3. Then, calculate the difference between each *T* score and the mean you have calculated.

This difference is statistically significant if it equals or exceeds the typeset number in the column labeled *H/L* in the Summary Table. The score is then likely to be higher, or lower, than the respondent's own mean on that composite or on the ESI; chances are fairly high—90%—that this is so. Write *H* for higher, or *L* for lower, on the line provided.

Two ESI *T* scores—Interpersonal Relations and Self-Esteem—require an additional step. Before making comparisons, invert the ESI mean by subtracting it from 100. The difference (100 minus the mean) is the *inverted mean.* If the mean is small, the inverted mean will be large, and vice versa. Next, compare the ESI *T* scores in question with the inverted mean. Use the original *T* scores, however, not the inverted ones. That is, compare the uninverted scale *T* scores with the inverted mean *T* score. For the remaining ESI *T* scores, use the original, uninverted mean.

Comparing the School and Clinical Maladjustment Composites. The School Maladjustment Composite and the Clinical Maladjustment Composite can be compared simply. Transfer the *T* scores for these composites from the rounded boxes to the rectangle labeled *Composite Comparison.* Calculate the difference between scores and enter it on the line marked *Difference* in the rectangle.

To the right of this line are two typeset numbers. If the difference equals or exceeds at least one of these numbers, circle the largest number that it equals or exceeds. The difference is statistically significant at the level indicated (for example, .05). Smaller significance levels represent greater chances that the first composite score is greater, or lesser, than the second.

Consult Appendix B for the percentage of people in the norming sample who have a difference as great as or greater than the examinee's. Last, indicate the direction of any statistically significant difference with the symbol > or <. Enter ≈ if the difference is statistically nonsignificant.

Recording Critical Items

On the Summary Page, place a check beside each critical item endorsed. These items may be important in their own right and may require follow-up.

The Parent and Teacher Report Forms

The scoring of the Parent Rating Scales (PRS) and Teacher Rating Scales (TRS) is similar to that of the SRP. This section covers departures from SRP scoring but does not repeat the bulk of the scoring instructions given already for the SRP.

The SRP versus the PRS and TRS

The SRP provides only two response options, *true* and *false,* but the PRS and TRS provide four: *never, sometimes, often,* and *almost always.* This difference changes the look of the Item Scoring Page. In addition, the design of the Summary Page is somewhat different for the rating scale protocols. The F column appears to the left, rather than the right, of the Clinical Profile. Finally, examiners do not need to invert any score by subtracting it from 100.

The most important differences involve the scales and composites themselves. The PRS and TRS contain scales that the SRP does not, and vice versa. The PRS and TRS have no L or V index. The three composites on the PRS and TRS are the Externalizing Composite, the Internalizing Composite, and the Adaptive Skills Composite. A Behavioral Symptoms Index (BSI) replaces the ESI.

These variations call for differences in interpretation, but the scoring of the three BASC protocols is essentially the same. With all protocols, for example, responses that contribute to the F index appear in the shaded area of the Item Scoring Page. The F score is always obtained by counting the number of shaded numbers circled.

Departures from the Self-Report of Personality Protocol

Two scoring differences do distinguish the SRP. If an examinee's father has completed a preschool- or child-level PRS, add 3 points to the Social Skills T score

Rapid Reference 3.6

PRS and TRS Scales That Tend to Show Sex Differences in Raw Scores

Higher Scores for Females
- Social Skills
- Study Skills
- Leadership
- Depression

Higher Scores for Males
- Aggression
- Conduct Problems
- Hyperactivity
- Attention Problems
- Learning Problems

before recording it in the Summary Table. Fathers tend to give lower ratings than mothers do on this scale. The correction makes the scores comparable for fathers and mothers.

On the TRS-C and TRS-A, examiners can compare three composites—Externalizing Problems, Internalizing Problems, and School Problems—rather than two. Thus, three comparisons, rather than one, are possible. The results are adjusted for multiple comparisons.

Finally, gender breakdowns for the scales depart from the SRP. The PRS and TRS show sex differences on the scales listed in Rapid Reference 3.6.

INTERPRETING BASC RESULTS

The Self-Report of Personality

The BASC SRP is designed to assess children's and adolescents' self-reports of their personalities. The form provided for adolescents incorporates three indexes not found in the children's form. Somatization and Sensation Seeking are clinical scales, whereas the L Index is a validity scale. The item content of the two forms also differs somewhat. These distinctions reflect differing research results for children and adolescents in the development of the BASC. Despite these few differences, the two inventories have largely the same structure. Examiners may interpret them in the same way for the two groups of young people.

A thorough understanding of the SRP (or any BASC protocol) is instrumental to proficient interpretation. The SRP samples symptomatology addressed by the *Diagnostic and Statistical Manual of Mental Disorders,* 4th ed. (*DSM-IV*) and by similar manuals, as well as by the 14 constructs found in Table 3.4.

This protocol also provides three validity scales. A treatment of the validity scales appears here, followed by a treatment of the 14 clinical and developmental scales.

The SRP scales quantify young people's reports of their thoughts, feelings, and perceptions. The scales represent multiple aspects of adaptiveness and maladaptiveness, particularly emotional disturbance. Thus, both positive and negative aspects of personality are represented. Because the SRP solicits reports from young people themselves, it yields insights that the Teacher and Parent Rating Scales cannot. Conversely, the rating scales provide the more reliable and objective results that adult observers make possible. In addition, the Student Observation System and the Structured Developmental History can inform interpretations of the SRP for increased comprehensiveness.

Validity Scales

The F Index

Respondents who obtain high scores on the *F* or *fake bad* scale have responded *true* or *false* to items that rarely elicit this response in the normative population. In doing so, they may have self-reported an unrealistically high number of symptoms or a pattern of symptoms that does not reflect any known disorder. *F* index scores in the Caution range may require investigation. Scores in the Extreme Caution range may affect interpretations of the remaining scales.

Validity indexes of this type are often called infrequency indexes and are thought to reflect an attempt by respondents to appear disturbed or pathological. Some respondents, however, may elevate the *F* index for other reasons. They may be in acute psychological distress; their responses may be an attempt to communicate this distress and obtain help. Unwillingness to cooperate or difficulty with the test form may also elevate the *F* scale. Thus, examiners should investigate such results before reaching conclusions. Interviewing respondents on the information covered by the items can help determine why they responded as they did. The individual conducting the interview should be alert for possible malingering.

The L Index

Like the *F* index, the *L* index consists of items to which few individuals in the norming sample made a specified response. The *L* index, however, is a *fake good* rather than *fake bad* index. On the SRP-A, a high L score may indicate defensiveness or unawareness of one's own behavior and feelings, an idealized presentation of the self, difficulty with the test form, or uncooperativeness. L scores in the Caution range may require investigation. Scores in the Extreme Caution range require investigation and nearly always invalidate the remainder of a profile. The SRP-C does not include an L index because high scores are common among children and often appear to reflect ordinary childhood characteristics (Reynolds & Kamphaus, 1998).

The V Index

Respondents obtaining high scores on the V index have endorsed nonsensical items. Possible reasons include carelessness and difficulty understanding test items. As shown in Table 3.5, even relatively low V index scores were rare in the norming sample. A V score of 2 renders validity questionable, and a V score of 3 or more, highly questionable. A score of 3 or more typically indicates uncooperativeness, illiteracy, mental retardation, confusion, or even psychosis (Reynolds & Kamphaus, 1998). The content of these items is typically more reflective of thought disorder than of depression.

Other Validity Indicators

In addition to high validity scores, other considerations may render SRP results questionable. One example is patterned responding. A respondent may

Table 3.5 V Scores and Their Frequencies and Percentages in the Norming Sample

V Score	Frequency	Percentage
0	3,831	75.3
1	853	16.8
2	208	4.1
3	111	2.2
4	56	1.1
5	23	0.5
6	4	0.1

mark T's alone or F's alone, may alternate T's and F's, or may produce a long series of T's followed by a long series of F's. The Item Scoring Page should be examined for these and other arbitrary patterns.

Large numbers of omitted items can render the results invalid. In the norming sample, 94% of respondents omitted four or fewer items on the SRP. A follow-up interview may suggest that a respondent needs assistance with these items. Alternatively, the content of the omitted items may suggest a reluctance to reveal information about certain topics. With some children or adolescents, an examiner may be able to obtain additional responses in an interview through encouragement and reassurance, or by carefully broaching these topics with the respondent.

A referred child or adolescent can sometimes make responses that do not indicate any problems. If other sources suggest that problems exist, examiners should consider the possibility of a positive response set. In addition, a careful review of educational records may provide evidence for limited English reading proficiency. A respondent may have a reading disorder, a first language other than English, or a history of low educational achievement (Reynolds & Kamphaus, 1998; Sattler, 1992).

Clinical Scales

Anxiety

The Anxiety scale assesses oversensitivity; irrational or excessive worries that typically are poorly defined in the respondent's mind; and *generalized fears,* or fears that extend beyond the specific sources previously associated with them. High scores on this scale may indicate a sense of dread; obsessive, intrusive, and bothersome thoughts, which if clinically significant may interfere with decision making; or other obsessive-compulsive features, such as ritualistic and perseverative behavior.

A T score below 41 may indicate an inflated sense of well-being. Such a score, coupled with a high sensation-seeking result, may predict later Conduct Disorder. An absence of anxiety over the harmful effects of one's behavior is a widely accepted indication of sociopathy, which often takes the form of Conduct Disorder in children and adolescents. This disorder can develop later into Antisocial Personality Disorder, which is quite difficult to treat effectively.

T scores of 60 to 64, the at-risk range, may denote chronic or acute distress.

People with chronic anxiety can feel overburdened by minor, day-to-day mishaps and can be prone to stress reactions. *T* scores of 65 or higher, the clinically significant range, indicate the clear presence of emotional or psychological distress and a tendency to respond negatively to one's environment. People with high degrees of anxiety may develop rigid patterns of thought and, in extreme cases, may become confused and disoriented. They may be hypersensitive to criticism and may interpret small slights as major letdowns or insults.

Anxiety scale results have shown high correlations with the *F*, Depression, and Anxiety (A and Psychasthenia) scales of the Minnesota Multiphasic Personality Inventory (MMPI). Respondents with high scores on the Anxiety scale tend to have low ego strength as measured by the MMPI (Reynolds & Kamphaus, 1998).

Attitude to School

This scale samples respondents' general opinion of the utility of school and degree of comfort with school-related experiences. The scale correlates highly with the Attitude to Teachers scale. Because scores on the latter may fluctuate in response to experiences with a teacher or school administrator (as noted below), Attitude to School scores may fluctuate concomitantly.

Scores of 40 or lower indicate that a respondent is relatively satisfied and comfortable with school. At-risk scores, 60 to 69, indicate a discomfort with most or all aspects of the school experience, except relationships with peers. A clinically significant score—70 or higher—suggests an increased risk of dropping out, especially if the respondent obtains a low Interpersonal Relations score and high Sensation Seeking and Sense of Inadequacy scores.

Respondents with high scores on the Attitude to School index may have added difficulties. Young children and females may tend to internalize and to have somatic complaints. Adolescent males can show externalizing behavior problems and display some antisocial behavior (Reynolds & Kamphaus, 1998).

Attitude to Teachers

This scale assesses perceptions of teachers as uncaring, unfair, or unmotivated to help their students. Scores may fluctuate in reaction to recent conflicts with or special help from a teacher or school administrator.

Low scores indicate a high regard for teachers. At-risk scores, 60 to 69, indicate dissatisfaction with teachers. Clinically significant scores, 70 or higher, indicate that the respondent is dissatisfied with teachers in most or all respects. Adolescents may be at increased risk of quitting school if a score of 70 or higher accompanies a low Interpersonal Relations score and high Attitude to School, Sensation Seeking, and Sense of Inadequacy scores. By contrast, if none of the latter four scores is high, and the Attitude to School score is in the typical range, the examiner should investigate the possibility of personality conflicts with particular teachers (Reynolds & Kamphaus, 1998).

Atypicality

This scale on the SRP assesses for unusual perceptions, thoughts, and behaviors commonly associated with severe forms of pathology such as thought disorders and psychosis. The items sample such symptoms as auditory and visual hallucinations, unusual sensory experiences, paranoid thoughts, and loss of control. At-risk or clinically significant scores may indicate confused thought patterns and an inability to exercise rational control over one's behavior.

At-risk Atypicality scores, 60 to 69, may indicate confused thought and possibly decompensation, as is associated with thought disorder. This scale in particular, however, should be interpreted with caution. A score of 60 or higher may reflect, in part, impulsivity, anxiety, or simply a realistic assessment of the examinee's adverse circumstances. Thus, several interpretations are possible. In addition, the real circumstances reflected in some items can be important in themselves. Examiners should therefore study individual item responses carefully and allow them to guide the process of interpretation.

Scores of 70 or higher on a valid SRP profile may be associated with serious thought disorders, developing or developed schizophrenia, and poor ego strength. Other possible interpretations include social alienation and a highly individualistic lifestyle on the part of a respondent's family. A score of 70 or higher always merits serious consideration as a possible indicator of severe emotional and mental disturbance.

If an adolescent obtains a high Atypicality score, particularly when accompanied by a high Sensation Seeking score, a review of possible alcohol or drug use should follow. Younger children with high Atypicality scores may be shy and introverted; peers and adults may view their behavior as highly individualized.

When atypicality is present, important considerations arise. Examiners should assist examinees and peers in keeping such behavior in perspective. Respondents who do not have a serious condition may display some atypical symptoms. In addition, peers may become aware of a respondent's atypical behavior and their negative reactions can create added difficulties. Students may be stereotyped and labeled as crazy, for example. Education of peers in the classroom can produce great benefits when atypicality is an issue.

Examiners themselves are not immune to overreactions or unintended stereotypes associated with atypicality. Self-awareness is important when working with atypical children and young people. The SRP Atypicality score correlates moderately with the Schizophrenia index and the Anxiety factor on the MMPI.

Depression

This scale assesses depressive symptoms, including feelings of loneliness and sadness and an inability to enjoy life. Many items reflect a sense of hopelessness, pessimism, and dread. Additional influences on this scale include anxiety and stress.

T scores of 60 to 69, the at-risk range, indicate considerable depression. T scores of 70 or higher, the clinically significant range, indicate broad problems with adjustment. Observers may overlook these problems because depressed children and adolescents are notably unintrusive.

Children and adolescents with high Depression scores often appear reserved or introverted to other people but show evidence of anxiety and emotional lability. These young people take few chances and may appear agitated at times. They often have difficulty relating to other people and expressing emotions at home, at school, and with peers. Adolescents with depression may have periods of anger and acting out. Because these problems appear in several environments, high scores on the SRP Depression scale should be compared with Depression ratings on the TRS and PRS (Reynolds & Kamphaus, 1998; Beck, 1967, 1976).

Locus of Control

This scale assesses respondents' perceptions of who or what controls the events of their lives. Low scores denote an internal locus of control, that is, a perception of having control over one's own success or failure. High scores denote an external locus of control, a perception that one's success or failure depends on forces beyond one's control. Research indicates that people's control beliefs regarding people in general correspond to their control beliefs regarding themselves. For example, individuals who think that people can control their own success or failure are likely to view themselves as having control of their own success or failure. In addition, locus of control correlates positively with success in school and with a positive outlook.

Respondents who obtain high scores on this scale have a sense of helplessness, an attitude that there is no point in trying. They may believe strongly in luck. They tend to place the blame for their problems on other people, including peers, parents, and teachers. In addition, they tend to expect that they will not be rewarded consistently or appropriately even when they behave as expected.

T scores of 60 to 69, the at-risk range, indicate a clearly established external locus of control. With a T score of 70 or higher, the clinically significant range, locus of control takes on greater connotations of pathology. Motivation may be compromised, along with the sense of controlling one's destiny, which plays a general role in psychological well-being. People obtaining these very high scores may have a mild paranoia about the world around them. They may view the world as irrational and unjust and may have commensurate feelings of anxiety or depression. Feelings of safety and security may be reduced (Reynolds & Kamphaus, 1998).

Recent victims of trauma and people with Post-traumatic Stress Disorder may obtain high scores on the Locus of Control scale. Pervasive mental health difficulties may also be associated with high scores (Reynolds & Kamphaus, 1998).

Sensation Seeking

Sensation seeking is a need for sensory stimulation and a willingness to take physical and social risks to obtain it. The adolescent form of the SRP incorporates a Sensation Seeking scale that assesses the desire to engage in exciting or potentially hazardous activities. This trait undoubtedly has adaptive value but often interferes with school achievement and behavior that is considered appropriate in contemporary society.

Researchers have found gender and age differences in sensation seeking. Males score higher than females, and the trait appears to peak in late adolescence and young adulthood (Reynolds & Kamphaus, 1998).

Respondents with T scores of 40 or lower are often seen as cautious, anxious, inhibited, and overcontrolled. *T* scores of 60 to 69, representing the at-risk range, indicate a tendency to be easily bored, to have high energy levels, and to engage in risky and potentially delinquent behavior. School conduct problems may often occur. The potential to experiment with or use alcohol and drugs increases in this range. In individuals with scores of 70 or higher, the clinically significant range, all of these behaviors are more likely. The probability of delinquent conduct increases.

High Sensation Seeking scores, especially when accompanied by low Anxiety scores, tend to be associated with a diagnosis of Conduct Disorder. Sensation Seeking has not, however, been associated with Attention-Deficit/Hyperactivity Disorder. The Sensation Seeking scale is part of the School Maladjustment composite because it correlates highly with school behavior problems and negative attitudes toward teachers and schooling in general.

Sense of Inadequacy

This scale assesses low belief in the ability to achieve at expected levels; a tendency not to persevere; and a self-perception of being unsuccessful, especially in academic pursuits. Respondents may feel too inadequate to meet expectations set by themselves or by other people. Individuals who set or accept unrealistically high goals for themselves would be likely to score high on this scale. The Sense of Inadequacy scale, then, is conceptually related to the concept of level of aspiration.

T scores of 60 to 69 denote mildly to moderately reduced confidence. *T* scores of 70 or higher indicate a respondent who feels unable to compete in the mainstream of society, one who may have given up to go his or her own way and who chooses not to pursue traditional goals.

Individuals with high Sense of Inadequacy scores tend to lack persistence and to reject the traditional goals of society. They may profess a devotion to alternative lifestyles or to alienated social groups. They may seem self-assured, but they often show some evidence of depression or anxiety, unless Conduct Disorder or Antisocial Personality Disorder is present. Younger children who score high may appear reserved, and others may view them as intellectually dull. A penchant for individualism may be evident even at ages 8–11 years.

Social Stress

This scale assesses stress in relation to the respondent's interactions with others. Social stress evokes feelings of pressure and tension and is associated with a lack of coping resources, especially the outlets afforded by close friends and social contact. Social Stress as measured on the SRP is likely to be pervasive and chronic, whereas other conceptualizations of stress emphasize an acute, transient presentation.

T scores of 60 to 69, the at-risk range, may reflect difficulties involving anxiety, confusion, and somatic complaints. Young children with scores of 70 or higher may turn inward in an unsuccessful attempt to cope with those difficulties. They may display shyness and proneness to guilt, along with emotional lability and an unexplained edginess or hyperirritability.

Somatization

This scale assesses a tendency to complain about relatively minor physical problems, with underlying psychological problems thought to be the true cause of the examinee's distress. The scale reflects the nature and degree of a series of health-related problems, fears, and concerns. Physical symptoms may be experienced as real or imaginary, but these complaints, if a sufficient number are endorsed, are likely to be *psychogenic,* that is, psychological in origin. Young children report these symptoms unreliably, but adolescents respond clearly to questions about somatization.

T scores of 60 to 69, the at-risk range, reflect anxiety, internalization, and repression of feeling. Chronic complaining may also be evident. With *T* scores of 70 or higher, the clinically significant range, hysteria may occur, histrionic displays may be relatively common, and serious physical ailments (e.g., ulcers) may develop. Also common at clinically significant levels is poor ego strength. If the Personal Adjustment composite is significantly low, examiners might consider a diagnosis of Identity Disorder, provided that other criteria are met.

Adaptive Scales

The BASC measures desirable characteristics in addition to the clinical characteristics most often measured by personality tests. In contrast with the Clinical scales, the Adaptive scales measure constructs that indicate healthy adjustment. High scores represent desirable characteristics. Although other tests also combine measures of both adaptive and maladaptive behaviors, most such tests have conceptual or statistical limitations (Sattler, 1992).

Interpersonal Relations

This scale assesses a respondent's self-reports of success and enjoyment attained in relating to other people. *T* scores of 31 to 40 indicate difficulty relating to other people and developing social skills. *T* scores of 30 or lower suggest the possibility of significant problems, primarily with peers. Problems with adults are also quite likely for respondents with an additional at-risk or clinically significant score on the Attitude to Teachers or Relations with Parents scale. Respondents scoring 30 or lower may be withdrawn and may lack the energy for social interaction, especially with a high Depression score (Reynolds & Kamphaus, 1998).

These respondents may intrude into others' interactions, however, prompting adverse reactions from them. Very low scorers tend to be prone to guilt, blaming themselves for a lack of success. These young people desire good interpersonal relations but are frustrated in their efforts to achieve them.

Relations with Parents

This scale surveys the respondents' perceptions of the degree of parental trust and concern, their self-perceptions of their importance in the family, and the status of the parent-child relationship. High scores denote good adjustment.

T scores of 31 to 40 indicate mildly to moderately disturbed relations with parents. Scores of 30 or lower suggest the possibility of severe family problems and perhaps alienation. At these very low scores, Conduct Disorder may be common. Adolescents may be very active and prone to act out. Younger children may more often appear reserved or show a feeling of inadequacy. Emotional lability and negative attitudes may be common.

Self-Esteem

This scale assesses respondents' satisfaction with their appearance, personality, and other characteristics. The scale is an important component of the Personal Adjustment composite. High scores denote self-esteem. Respondents with high scores may appear to observers to be warm, open, venturesome, and self-assured. Typically, their peer relations are strong, their sense of their own identity is positive, and their ego strength is at adaptive levels.

Individuals with low Self-Esteem scores, especially below 30, tend to display dissatisfaction with most or all aspects of the self. Shyness, anxiety, depression, and a feeling of tension occur frequently. For young people with low self-esteem, an atmosphere of trust and acceptance is crucial to the intervention process. Heavily confrontational or directive approaches may exacerbate the respondent's presenting problems.

Self-Reliance

This scale assesses assurance of one's ability to make decisions and to act independently with confidence. High scorers tend to take responsibility and to face life's challenges. These respondents tend not to be fearful of their emotions and have strong internal control.

T scores of 40 or lower may indicate low self-confidence; difficulty in facing challenges, especially emotionally difficult ones; and a tendency to repress unpleasant thoughts or feelings. Shyness and internalization are common, along with a basic insecurity. Younger respondents may show relatively high dependence and separation anxiety.

Results with the norming sample indicate that this scale is a strong measure of personal adjustment. The Self-Reliance scale has a substantial negative correlation of –.53 with the MMPI Repression factor (Reynolds & Kamphaus, 1998).

Composites

Compared with scores from particular scales, composite scores are typically more consistent—over time, for example—and less susceptible to chance fluctuations. In addition, they are better measures and predictors of the intended constructs. Unlike the scale scores of the SRP, which help to identify specific difficulties or strengths, the SRP composite scores are helpful in summarizing responses and reaching general conclusions about broad areas of functioning and adaptation.

Two composites address maladjustment: adjustment and symptoms. Nevertheless, psychological tests have no inherent direction. They can be seen as reversible: A maladjustment scale is merely an adjustment scale scored in reverse. Thus, a low School Maladjustment score and a high Personal Adjustment score, for example, may be interpreted comparably and may be seen as mutually consistent within the limits imposed by their differing content.

Reverse scoring is more useful for some scales than for others. It is largely beside the point for the Emotional Symptoms index; there is little to gain by interpreting this scale as a measure of the absence of symptoms. When consulting its subtests and items, an examiner may nevertheless find their reversible quality informative.

Clinical Maladjustment

This composite includes the Anxiety, Atypicality, Locus of Control, and Social Stress scales. For adolescents, the Clinical Maladjustment composite also includes Somatization. This composite is a broad index of distress reflecting clinical, internalizing problems.

A respondent who has average scores on all individual SRP scales may nevertheless have a high score on the Clinical Maladjustment composite because of the cumulative effect of difficulties in multiple areas. This composite, then, can help to identify respondents who may be having serious difficulties that specific scales do not detect.

T scores of 60 to 69 on the Clinical Maladjustment composite warrant careful consideration. Scores of 70 or higher almost certainly indicate substantial difficulties. A respondent with a high Clinical Maladjustment score and a low Personal Adjustment score may be relatively vulnerable and may have few coping resources. A careful evaluation, then, is essential, and intervention should be prompt (Reynolds & Kamphaus, 1998).

School Maladjustment

This composite includes the Attitude to School and Attitude to Teachers scales, and for adolescents, Sensation Seeking. The manual (Reynolds & Kamphaus, 1998) describes this composite as a broad measure of adaptation to school. Schooling and relationships in the school setting constitute a large and influential part of a young person's life, and school difficulties are likely to reflect in environments outside the school.

High scores on this composite indicate a pattern of dissatisfaction with many aspects of schooling, school personnel, and the structure of the educational process. Examiners should investigate T scores of 60 to 69 because respondents scoring in this range sometimes have academic difficulties. Clinically significant T scores of 70 and above are most often associated with serious problems with schooling and in the school environment. Adolescent respondents with such problems may be at risk of dropping out. In addition, pervasive difficulties with schooling rarely occur in the absence of other personal and emotional difficulties.

Personal Adjustment

This composite consists of the Relations with Parents, Interpersonal Relations, Self-Reliance, and Self-Esteem scales. High scores denote good adjustment.

At-risk T scores, 31 to 40, suggest difficulty with interpersonal relationships, self-acceptance, identity development, and ego strength. Respondents scoring in this range tend toward withdrawal and repression of uncomfortable feelings and thoughts. They are likely to have few constructive outlets for sharing their problems. Respondents with clinically significant scores of 30 or lower frequently have insufficient coping skills and inadequate support systems. Scores in both of these ranges often suggest disturbed relations with peers (Reynolds & Kamphaus, 1998).

The combination of a low Personal Adjustment composite score and a high Clinical Maladjustment composite score indicates that difficulties are likely and that support and effective coping strategies are weak. Low scores on this composite are more likely to correlate with adjustment disorders and with certain Axis II personality disorders than with the more clinical syndromes associated with high Clinical Maladjustment scores.

Emotional Symptoms Index

The ESI, technically an additional composite, is a wide-ranging indicator of serious emotional disturbance, particularly internalizing disorders. It consists of the Anxiety and Social Stress scales of the Clinical Maladjustment composite; the Interpersonal Relations and Self-Esteem scales of the Personal Adjustment composite; and two additional scales, Depression and Sense of Inadequacy.

Elevated ESI scores almost always indicate serious emotional disturbance widely affecting the respondent's thoughts and feelings. Like the Clinical Maladjustment composite, the ESI can produce high scores in response to a cumulation of items that in isolation would not be considered serious. Nevertheless, respondents with high scores on the ESI often also have high scores on several of its component scales and on at least one other composite (Reynolds & Kamphaus, 1998).

A T score of 31 to 40 for a referred client often represents denial or socially desirable fabrication. The examiner should review results of the validity indexes. T scores of 65 to 69 indicate clear, pervasive distress. Valid scores of 70 and higher nearly always suggest serious emotional disturbance in some form. When investigating the nature of such disturbance, a careful examination of the SRP scales that do not contribute to the ESI is useful, as is a comparison with the BASC Teacher and Parent Rating Scales and with the Structured Developmental History.

SAD Triad

Three ESI scales—Social Stress, Anxiety, and Depression (SAD)—merit a conjoint examination. High scores on these three scales suggest severe emotional disturbance characterized by depression, tension, and distress. If all three *T* scores are 65 or higher, the possibility of a suicide risk warrants consideration, especially with an adolescent respondent. An approaching decompensation process is also possible. A valid SAD profile should evoke special attention and a follow-up interview and assessment.

Critical Items

The SRP includes a limited number of critical items taken to merit concern in their own right. Most of these items suggest suicidal ideation, feelings of hopelessness or worthlessness, experiences or behaviors that are out of the respondent's control, danger to the respondent or to others, or need for referral. These items should not be considered highly reliable or valid. Rather, they serve as a starting point for additional investigation. The examiner should probe these items and consider possible follow-up (Reynolds & Kamphaus, 1998).

Summary

The BASC SRP scales represent multiple aspects of adaptiveness and maladaptiveness. The SRP solicits reports from young people themselves, yielding insights that the Teacher and Parent Rating Scales cannot. Conversely, the rating scales contribute reliability and objectivity. Other sources of information, such as the Student Observation System and the Structured Developmental History, can guide interpretations of the SRP for greater comprehensiveness. Interpretation of the SRP requires a thorough understanding of its properties.

THE PARENT AND TEACHER RATING SCALES

The BASC PRS and TRS assess children's and adolescents' behavior in the home, school, and community. The two scales are very similar and clinicians can use them to provide complementary profiles based on respondents' differing opportunities to observe a young person's behavior. This section covers interpretation of the scales when it differs from that of the SRP (addressed previously) or when necessary for continuity. Differences occur primarily in the composition of subtests, and therefore of composites.

The PRS and TRS sample the symptomatology addressed by the *Diagnostic and Statistical Manual of Mental Disorders*, 4th ed. (*DSM-IV*) and by similar manuals, as well as the 14 constructs found in Table 3.2. A validity scale, the *F* index, accompanies these scales. This section presents the *F* index and other validity indicators, followed by the 14 clinical and developmental scales.

The PRS and TRS scales quantify adults' observations of young people's behavior. The scales represent multiple aspects of externalizing and internalizing behavior, both of which have had long-standing empirical support. The two instruments also measure adaptive skills; thus, they sample both positive and negative aspects of behavior.

Validity Indicators

The **F** Index

A high *F* or fake bad score for a young person may indicate either unrealistically negative ratings by the respondent or extremely maladaptive behavior by the young person. *F* index scores in the Caution or Extreme Caution range may require investigation. Scores in the Extreme Caution range may indicate that a negative response set has skewed the remaining PRS or TRS.

Other Validity Indicators

As with the SRP, considerations other than validity scores may render PRS or TRS results questionable. Patterned responding on these protocols may, for example, take the form of a long series of *N*s followed by a long series of *S*s. Large numbers of omitted items can render the results invalid. In the standardization sample, 97% of parents and 94% of teachers omitted four or fewer items on the PRS and TRS, respectively.

Ratings for a referred child or adolescent may not indicate any problems. If other sources suggest that problems exist, examiners should consider the possibility of a positive response set. Finally, a careful review of background information may provide evidence for limited English reading proficiency.

Examiners can compare the ratings to other BASC results to assess for invalidity. TRS results are likely to be accurate if, for example, they are similar to PRS results or to the TRS ratings of other educational professionals. On the other hand, invalidity is likely if TRS results differ from these additional ratings. An alternative explanation for differing results is that the young person may have situation-specific difficulties.

Clinical Scales

The relatively brief guidelines for the TRS and PRS Clinical Scales reflect the lesser amount of information available as yet for these scales, as compared with the Clinical Scales of the SRP.

Aggression
This scale on the TRS and PRS assesses both (a) verbal aggression, such as name-calling, blaming, and verbal threats, and (b) physical aggression, such as breaking others' possessions, hitting people, and being cruel to animals. The scale gives greater weight to verbal aggression because it occurs more frequently than physical aggression.

T scores of 60 or above tend to occur for young people with disruptive behavior disorders: Attention-Deficit/Hyperactivity Disorder (ADHD), Conduct Disorder, and Oppositional Defiant Disorder. Clinically significant aggression scores indicate highly disruptive behavior that may be of great concern to teachers, parents, and other caregivers. The Aggression scale clusters with other measures of Externalizing Problems.

Anxiety
The Anxiety scale assesses nervousness, excessive worry, fears and phobias, and self-deprecation. Young people with anxiety disorders typically present with additional symptoms, such as somatic complaints. Thus, elevated Anxiety and Somatization scores may be more appropriate than an elevated Anxiety score alone to evaluate a young person on *DSM-IV* criteria for Separation Anxiety Disorder, Overanxious Disorder, or Avoidant Disorder. Anxiety is a common symptom of other disorders, such as Depression and ADHD.

Attention Problems
The Attention Problems scale and the Hyperactivity scale were designed to aid in the diagnosis of ADHD, a condition characterized by hyperactivity, impul-

sivity, and inattention. The scale measures inability to maintain attention and distractibility from tasks that place demands on attention.

The Attention Problems scale is essential to the diagnosis of ADHD. This scale may also be useful in itself, aiding in the reliable diagnosis of attention deficit without hyperactivity. Research shows a correlation of about .6 between the Attention Problems and Hyperactivity scales. In addition, Attention Problems does not load highly on the Externalizing Problems factor, so young people may be inattentive without displaying externalizing behavior. This scale is part of the School Problems composite on the TRS.

Atypicality

This scale on the PRS or TRS may assess atypicality to some extent, but atypical disorders are rare among young people, particularly children. A *T* score of 60 or higher on this scale may also indicate immaturity, developmental delay, or a disruptive behavior disorder. The atypicality scale samples such behaviors as rocking, chewing clothing, babbling to oneself, and eating nonfood items. These behaviors are rare and potentially significant, so a *T* score of 60 or higher merits a careful item examination.

Conduct Problems

This scale, not found on the PRS, assesses socially deviant and disruptive behaviors that are characteristic of Conduct Disorder. The items cover such behaviors as stealing, lying, cheating in school, running away from home, and use of drugs and alcohol.

A young person with an at-risk Conduct Problems score of 60 or above may also have high scores on other scales, such as Learning Problems and Depression. The Conduct Problems and Aggression scales are closely related but measure different constructs. The former focuses on rule breaking and antisocial behavior and the latter examines behaviors directed against other people.

Depression

This scale on the PRS assesses *DSM-IV* criteria for depression, including depressed mood, suicidal ideation, self-reproach, and withdrawal. Many of these items assess depressive cognitions about self, world, and future (Beck, 1967, 1976), and are therefore written in quotation form (e.g., *Says, "Nobody understands me."*).

Groups with at-risk scores of 60 or above on this scale include those diagnosed with Depression, Conduct Disorder, and Behavior Disorder. Depressive symptoms occur with many other conditions, including anxiety disorders and Conduct Disorder.

Hyperactivity

The TRS and PRS Hyperactivity scale assesses hyperactivity and impulsivity. Behaviors measured by hyperactivity items include tapping the foot or a pencil, leaving one's seat during meals, and being overactive. Behaviors measured by impulsivity items include acting without thinking, rushing through assignments, and not waiting for one's turn in games and other activities.

The two sets of items make up one scale because hyperactivity and impulsivity were indistinguishable in factor analyses. Young people with ADHD are likely to have scores above 60 on Hyperactivity and Inattention, along with Aggression, Learning Problems, Conduct Problems, and Depression. Their Social Skills scores may be low.

Learning Problems

This scale of the TRS was developed to gather information from teachers for use in screening for or diagnosing learning disabilities or underachievement. Domains sampled by the Learning Problems scale include reading, writing, mathematics, and academic skills. A T score of 60 or above on this scale indicates the need for a careful investigation of academic skills.

Learning difficulties and learning disabilities often occur with disruptive behavior disorders such as Conduct Disorder and ADHD. An estimated 25% to 30% of ADHD children also have learning disabilities.

Somatization

This scale on the PRS and TRS assesses Somatization Disorder, which is characterized by numerous bodily complaints not due to poor physical health. These complaints typically persist for months or years. Somatization items on the BASC rating scales are drawn from *DSM-III-R* criteria and the research literature.

Withdrawal

This scale measures a tendency to avoid interpersonal and social contact. Mild withdrawal may be a symptom of depression. Withdrawal is associated also with neglect or rejection by peers. For elevated scores, the examiner may need to conduct a sociometric assessment to distinguish between neglected and rejected status. Rejected children are more likely to be lonely, to respond poorly to social skills training, and to experience depressive disorders later in life.

Clinically significant T scores of 70 and higher may suggest a possible pathological withdrawal similar to that found with autism. Withdrawal may be, but is not always, a symptom of depression. Correspondingly, the Withdrawal and Depression scales correlate only moderately.

Adaptive Scales

As with the SRP, Adaptive scales on the PRS and TRS assess constructs indicative of healthy adjustment. High scores represent desirable characteristics.

Adaptability
This scale assesses a young person's flexibility and capacity to adapt to changes. Adaptability items assess the ability to change tasks, to adjust to new teachers and changes in routine, and to share possessions with other children. Adaptability, based on temperament research, correlates with school achievement. Other temperament variables that also correlate with school achievement are activity level and distractibility.

Leadership
This scale assesses behaviors that may be related to leadership potential. Some Leadership items are related to Social Skills items; examples include the items addressing club membership or participation in extracurricular activities. Other Leadership items address cognitive skills related to problem solving.

Social Skills
This PRS and TRS scale focuses on interpersonal social activities, such as admitting mistakes, encouraging others, offering help, and saying *please* and *thank you*. A T score of 40 or lower may indicate a need for social skills training. The particular items endorsed specify behaviors that need improvement. In addition, research on the BASC, along with other research, suggests that socialization may be considerably more impaired for children diagnosed with autism than for those diagnosed with mental retardation. In clinical BASC samples, children with mild mental retardation obtained Social Skills scores about 1 standard deviation higher than a combined group of children and adolescents

with autism. Adolescents with mild mental retardation obtained scores about .66 standard deviations higher than the autistic group. The scores of high-functioning autistic children are still unknown but are likely to be below average.

Study Skills

This scale focuses on metamemory and learning strategies, and its items derive from research in these areas. Metacognitive behaviors assessed include note taking and analyzing problems before solving them. The scale also assesses organizational skills, including completing homework and reading assigned chapters. An examination of Study Skills items can suggest targets for behavioral and cognitive intervention.

A T score of 40 or lower may predict later behavioral problems. Failure to complete assignments, for example, may signal a more general decline in school performance, as seen with Depression or Conduct Disorder. The Study Skills scale has a substantial relationship to the School Problems composite, supporting the intuitively logical relationship between this scale and school adaptation (Reynolds & Kamphaus, 1998).

Composites

Like most composite scores, the BASC composite scores denote behavioral constructs that are distinct but that frequently occur together. Research on the BASC indicates sound construct validity (see Chapter 2 for a definition of this term).

Externalizing Problems

This composite incorporates the scales measuring Hyperactivity, Conduct Problems, and Aggression scales. Because externalizing problems are directed toward other people and the external environment, they are more obvious. Such problems typically are disruptive, evoking negative reactions more frequently than internalizing problems. They tend to suggest a less favorable prognosis.

Internalizing Problems

This composite incorporates the Depression, Anxiety, and Somatization scales. Unlike externalizing problems, internalizing problems are not disruptive. Young people with internalizing problems are typically compliant, controlled, self-monitoring. Their relationships may be impaired by withdrawal rather than disruption. Their problems often go unnoticed; therefore, detection of these difficulties is a priority. Young people with internalizing conditions can, however, show some externalizing behavior. An adolescent with depression can, for example, have difficulty with anger.

School Problems

Included in the child and adolescent TRS, this composite incorporates the Attention Problems and Learning Problems scale. The difficulties assessed include motivational, attentional, learning, and cognitive problems. A high score on this composite indicates behaviors that are very likely to impede academic achievement.

Adaptive Skills

This composite includes the Adaptability, Social Skills, and Leadership scales, and on the TRS, Study Skills. The Adaptive Skills T score is a summary of diverse adaptive skills, including social, organizational, and study skills. Young people's scores on this composite can be expected to correlate negatively with those on the other composites: Students with high scores on the Adaptive Skills composite have low scores on the Clinical scales, and students with low Adaptive Skills scores have high scores on the Clinical scales.

For some examinees, clinical problems interfere with adaptation, as when hyperactivity impairs an adolescent's study skills. Conversely, many adaptive skills appear to act as buffers against clinical problems. A child with high social skills, for example, is likely to have correspondingly lower withdrawal. Determining causes is extremely difficult in practice; practitioners therefore need to supplement their knowledge of research findings with clinical observation and judgment.

The Behavioral Symptoms Index

This composite takes in a combination of scales central to the Clinical composites. Thus, it measures overall problem behavior. Although selected from other composites, the Behavioral Symptoms index reflects a construct supported by scientific research, just as the other composites do.

Summary

The PRS and TRS reflect behavior observed in the young person's school and community. This section has addressed the meaning, utility, and interpretation of the scales and composites of these rating scale inventories. The rating scales complement the SRP to provide a comprehensive portrayal of strengths and difficulties that are central to the young person's personal and academic success.

🐟 TEST YOURSELF 🐟

1. **Readability statistics for the BASC PRS and the child and adolescent SRP indicate grade levels of _____, respectively.**
   - (a) 2.0, 2.0, and 3.0
   - (b) 4.0, 4.0, and 5.0
   - (c) 5.0, 3.0, and 7.0
   - (d) 9.0, 3.0, and 8.0

2. **The SRP is**
   - (a) a set of separate scales limited to measuring specific characteristics.
   - (b) an omnibus inventory, with scales that combine into an overall measure.
   - (c) a brief, 10-item scale that measures overall symptomatology.
   - (d) a 10-item scale that focuses on hyperactivity and related characteristics.

3. **The PRS and TRS measure numerous characteristics**
   - (a) but nonetheless take only about 10 to 20 minutes to administer.
   - (b) and therefore require about 60 to 70 minutes to administer.
   - (c) and administration time varies from 30 to 60 minutes.
   - (d) and administration time varies from 20 to 60 minutes.

4. **_____ may complete the TRS.**
   - (a) Any adult who has observed the child at length
   - (b) Any adult who has observed the child at length in a school, preschool, or similar setting
   - (c) Only a teacher or other educational professional
   - (d) Only a teacher

5. **For the Clinical scales of the BASC, _____ which items to sum when scoring.**

   (a) a color-coding scheme identifies
   (b) calculations determine
   (c) a scoring key lists
   (d) arrows show

6. **To find a composite score, you should**

   (a) consult Appendix G in the manual.
   (b) sum the T scores and enter the sum in the box beneath them.
   (c) sum the T scores and enter the sum into the appropriate formula.
   (d) list the L scores on the score conversion page and follow the instructions.

7. **In addition to comparing the child's scores on the School and Clinical Maladjustment Composites, you may also identify subtest scores that differ significantly from**

   (a) scores on individual items.
   (b) their respective composite means.
   (c) the overall mean for the inventory.
   (d) school grades and other external indices.

8. **Children with an elevated V index have endorsed nonsensical items and**

   (a) qualify for a diagnosis of Schizophrenia, frequently of the Paranoid Type.
   (b) may have responded carelessly or had trouble understanding the items.
   (c) have portrayed themselves in an unrealistically positive manner.
   (d) have attempted to appear deeply disturbed.

9. **For the BASC, interpretive information is**

   (a) not available because the instrument is very new.
   (b) becoming available for the most widely used scales.
   (c) now available for most Clinical and Adaptive scales.
   (d) available in the manual for each scale and composite.

10. **The SRP Personal Adjustment composite, a positive or adaptive measure, consists of which four scales?**

   (a) Self-Esteem, Self-Reliance, Interpersonal Relations, and Relations with parents
   (b) Self-Control, Self-Confidence, Internal Motivation, and Social Flexibility
   (c) Self-Control, Self-Monitoring, Industriousness, and Resilience
   (d) Self-Esteem, Self-Concept, Optimism, and Realism

Answers: 1. a; 2. b; 3. a; 4. b; 5. d; 6. b; 7. b; 8. b; 9. d; 10. a

Four

THE CHILD BEHAVIOR CHECKLIST AND RELATED INSTRUMENTS

The Child Behavior Checklist (CBCL) is designed for a parent to complete. Many related inventories accompany this one, including the Teacher Report Form (TRF), the Caregiver-Teacher Report Form (C-TRF), the Youth Self-Report (YSR), and the Young Adult Self-Report (YASR). For the TRF, a computer-scorable protocol is available in addition to the hand-scored protocol.

This chapter addresses the CBCL, the TRF, and the YSR. Achenbach (1997a, 1997b, respectively) provides information on the C-TRF and YASR. The CBCL is available in two versions, the CBCL/2-3 and CBCL/4-18, appropriate for ages 2 to 3 years and 4 to 18 years, respectively. The TRF is appropriate for ages 5 to 18 years, and the YSR, for ages 11 to 18 years. In addition, examinees completing the YSR should have at least fifth-grade reading skills and a mental age of 10 years. Rapid Reference 4.1 outlines publication information for the CBCL.

ADMINISTERING THE CHILD BEHAVIOR CHECKLIST

Initial Considerations

The CBCL forms are fairly clear and have response options next to the respective items. The items are alphabetized on the test form so that respondents may not guess their purpose and give biased responses as a result. The responses do not transfer automatically to the scoring sheet, however; they must be transferred by hand to columns at the bottom of the scoring form. A template is provided to facilitate this process. The scoring sheet is somewhat complex for busy practitioners; scoring requires considerable familiarity with the manual.

Achenbach (1991a) writes that most parents who have at least fifth-grade

≡Rapid Reference 4.1

Child Behavior Checklist (CBCL)

Author: Thomas Achenbach

Publication Date: 1991

What the test measures: Behavior problems.

Administration time: 20 min

Qualification of examiners: Graduate- or professional-level training in psychological assessment.

Publisher: University Associates in Psychiatry
Dept. of Psychiatry
University of Vermont
1 South Prospect Street
Burlington, VT 05401
802-656-8313
www.aseba.org

Prices: All items sold separately

reading skills can complete the CBCL. Completion typically takes 15–17 minutes. If a parent has reading limitations or other difficulties completing the CBCL, the following procedure is suggested: An interviewer hands the parent a copy of the protocol and retains a second copy. The interviewer says, "I'll read you the questions on this form and I'll write down your answers." Parents who have no difficulty reading the protocol typically begin to complete it on their own. Achenbach notes that this approach increases standardization by permitting all parents to view the format of the items during administration.

Parents who complete the protocol on their own should have the opportunity to request clarification. For respondents who do not speak English, the CBCL manual (Achenbach, 1991a) lists more than 30 languages in which translations are available. Parents may complete the CBCL at home or in a waiting room.

Appropriate Administration

Drotar, Stein, and Perrin (1995) raise the concern that examiners are administering the CBCL in regions where it has not been normed. We discourage this use because it leads to results that are distorted to an unknown degree. Any psychological test should be administered only to groups for whom it has been normed—for example, boys and girls in the United States, of any ethnicity, and between the ages of 12 and 18. A test normed for both sexes or for several ethnicities may have a separate profile form for each of these groups or a single form for all of them. A good examiner's manual clearly states which groups should take the test. Finally, clinicians can norm a test themselves for local populations, such as patients with a specified condition or students of specified SES levels in the local school district. Even if the test already has national norms, the new norms may result in more accurate scores.

A related issue is the purpose for which an examiner uses an instrument. Evidence from research should be available showing that the test is suited for a particular purpose. The best evidence comes from norming, whether at a national, regional, or local level. Evidence from published studies is apt, although often limited in its applications by sampling considerations. If a study uses the test's norming sample, however, it carries a good deal of weight.

Preparation

All Forms

Administering the CBCL is relatively easy, and difficult elements typically have a purpose. An exception lies with the blue form headed *Child Behavior Checklist for Ages 4–18* (or *2–3*), which should specify more clearly who is to complete it. Similar forms for three other versions are obviously meant for teachers, for either teachers or caregivers, and for young people themselves. The blue form is apparently meant for a parent or guardian because *Mother, Father,* and *Other* are the response options of an initial item. With this exception, the CBCL is self-explanatory.

The first part of the CBCL/4-18 contains two pages of background and history items, such as repeated grades and jobs or chores the child has. This section is scored and contains important information both for clinicians and for researchers. It therefore should be completed consistently for all children examined. This section does not appear on the CBCL/2-3 because most of its items do not apply to very young children.

The CBCL/2-3 contains 100 items. The main part of the CBCL/4-18 contains 120 items. The numbering reaches only 113 because several multipart items are counted as single items. Both inventories present open-ended items, which may tax the respondent. Some respondents may want to take a short break, depending on their physical or psychological constitution. The examiner might check in periodically or stay and watch for signs of fatigue or frustration.

The open-ended items can serve as validity checks, guarding against misinterpretation. Item 84 on the CBCL/4-18, for example, reads *Strange behavior (describe)*. This phrase may identify symptoms of thought disorder or simply behaviors that are rare or unusual. The written response to the item can be reviewed for clarification. Other items, such as *Trouble sleeping (describe)* can guide referral or help distinguish between problems with physical and emotional causes.

Rapport and Instructions

In administering the CBCL or any psychological test, examiners should convey competence and professionalism and should adhere to current standards of testing and test development (AERA, APA, & NCME, 1999). As noted for the BASC, examiners should honestly address parents' potential concerns, such as reasons for the evaluation, intended use of the results, limits of confidentiality, and applicable local laws.

Consistent with other instructions in the manual (Achenbach, 1991a), an interviewer might hand the protocol to the respondent and say, "I would like you to read the questions on this form and mark your answers. For items followed by a line, follow the brief instructions."

SCORING THE CHILD BEHAVIOR CHECKLIST

The Competence Scales and Composite

Items I–VII of the CBCL/4-18 are not simply background information; they combine to form three scales—the Activities, Social, and School

DON'T FORGET
....
Before scoring the CBCL/4-18, be familiar with Appendix A and the section entitled "Scoring the CBCL/4-18" in Chapter 12 of the manual. For the CBCL/2-3, see Appendix A and the section entitled "Scoring the CBCL/2-3" in Chapter 10 of the manual.

DON'T FORGET

Exclude any competence scale from scoring if data are missing from more than one of its items.

DON'T FORGET

Item I-A calls for parents to list the sports in which the child or adolescent most likes to participate. If a parent has listed 0 or 1 sport, score 0; if 2 sports, score 1; if 3 or more sports, score 2. Next, obtain the mean or sum of these scores, depending on the item. Obtain the mean by adding all scores for an item—all 0s, 1s, and 2s—then dividing by the number of scores. Enter the mean or sum on the reverse of the profile page.

scales—which in turn form a Competence composite. Each item in this section represents several items clustered together because of their similar content. Clinicians can interpret the scores on these scales along with the more conventional CBCL scales. Appendix A of the manual presents detailed, complex instructions for scoring these items. The profile for the Competence scale appears on the back of each CBCL/4-18 profile form.

Achenbach (1991a) notes a few scoring exceptions that examiners should know before proceeding. Do not score the competence scales for children aged 4 and 5 years. Do not score item II-A, *# of nonsports activities,* for any age group. You may, however, enter this score in the space provided on the profile form. Finally, do not score any competence scale if data are missing for more than one of the items that contribute to it. Exclude the Activities scale, for example, if more than one of its five scores are missing.

To proceed with scoring, first locate the appropriate profile form for the examinee's gender. Generally, score competence items as shown in Table 4.1. Score certain individual items, however, as noted in the following paragraph.

Table 4.1 General Rules for Scoring Items I–VII of the CBCL/4-18

Number Reported by Parent	Score
0 or 1	0
2	1
3 or more	2

Note. These guidelines should not be used uniformly with all items.

Table 4.2 Scoring of Item V-2, CBCL/4-18

Number Reported by Parent	Score
0 or 1	0
2 or 3	1
4 or more	2

Score item V-2, *contacts with friends,* as in Table 4.2. For item VII-2, *special class,* score 0 if the student is taking a remedial class or classes; if not, score 1. This item, then, is scored in reverse compared to most competence items. Also score items VII-3 and VII-4 in reverse. Enter these scores on the competence profile form on the opposite side of the CBCL/4-18 profile. Enter each score under *Activities, Social,* or *School,* as appropriate.

Calculate the scale scores as shown in Table 4.3. Then, plot the three scores in the competence profile plot—the large box above the columns where you have entered and summed the scores. To plot a score you have calculated, first note that within the box are two columns above the one where you entered the item scores. These columns represent ages 6–11 years and ages 12–18 years. Competence profiles apply only to these age ranges. Select the column representing the examinee's age range. Then locate the desired score and make an *X* over it. Connect the *X*s with straight lines; we suggest using a ruler or other straight edge. Finally, read to the left across the profile plot to obtain the percentile for each scale score. Read to the right to obtain the *T* score.

To obtain the Competence composite score, simply add the three scale

Table 4.3 Scoring the Three Competence Scales of the CBCL

Scale	Items to Sum	Rounding	If One Score Is Missing
Activities	5	Nearest .5	Use mean of other 4 scores
Social	6	Nearest .5	Use mean of other 5 scores
School	4	None	Do not score the scale

Note. Obtain the total competence score by summing the scores on the three scales. Enter this sum in the competence profile. Be sure to enter the sum in the column for the appropriate age range, 6–11 or 12–18.

scores. Three lines are provided to the right of the competence profile to enter and add the three scores. Write the sum on the fourth line. The table on the far right of the competence profile page lists T scores for this composite score.

Syndrome Scales and Other Problems

Ensure that you have the appropriate profile form for the examinee—the form for girls aged 4–18 years, for example. Also locate the appropriate templates. If data are missing for more than eight total items, do not score the CBCL/4-18 or 2-3. Exclude items 2, 4, 56h, and 113 on the CBCL/4-18, or 51, 79, and 100 on the CBCL/2-3, from scoring (Achenbach, 1991a).

If a parent has circled two numbers for an item, score 1 for that item. For the CBCL/2-3, only an informant who lives with the examinee should score items 12, 22, 28, 38, 48, 52, 64, 65, 74, 84, 94, and 95 (Achenbach, 1991a, 1992).

Some CBCL items are *open-ended:* They allow parents to write in their responses. Others are *closed-ended,* requiring parents to select from a limited number of options. On the CBCL inventories, a parent may write in a response that is covered already by a closed-ended item. Score only the closed-ended item, and score this item *even if the parent has not actually endorsed it.* The parent has indicated elsewhere that the item is applicable. In general, score only one item for a particular behavior. That item should be the one that refers most specifically to the behavior (Achenbach, 1991a, 1992). Table 4.4 presents parent responses that should be omitted from scoring, and Table 4.5 presents solutions to specific scoring situations.

The two templates for the CBCL/4-18 cover items 1–113—or 1–100 for

Table 4.4 Parent Responses to Be Omitted from CBCL Scoring

Item	Content	Responses to Be Omitted
9	Obsessions	Behaviors that are clearly not obsessional, such as "Keeps hitting sister"
40, 70	Hears sounds; sees things	Anxiety over real sights or sounds; experiences while under the influence of drugs or alcohol
28	Eats and drinks things that are not food	Names of sweets, junk food

Table 4.5 Solutions to Situations That May Occur during CBCL Scoring

Item or Behavior	Parent's Response	Scoring
Extreme behavior such as setting fires or attempting suicide	Parent writes that it happened but circles 0 or no number	Assign 1[a]
Any open-ended item	"Used to do this"	Score as parent did

[a]Exception: Behavior clearly occurred before the time specified in the rating instructions: >6 months ago, unless the user substitutes a different time.

CBCL/2-3—making these items relatively easy to score. Begin with the template for page 3, or page 1 for ages 2–3 years. The templates show roman numerals beside the item numbers, indicating the syndrome scale to which an item belongs.

On the profile form, find the column representing the scale you are scoring. In this column, write in the number circled by the parent—0, 1, or 2—next to the appropriate item number. If a parent circles *1* for item 47, which belongs to the Anxious/Depressed scale, enter *1* beside the number 47 under Anxious/Depressed.

Some items are not part of a syndrome scale. For them, the template indicates *Other Problems*. Enter scores on these items in the *Other Problems* column to the right of the syndrome scale columns. Sum these scores and include them in the total score for the CBCL/2-3, but not for the CBCL/4-18.

Repeat the scoring process using the template for the next page. Place the item scores in their respective columns on the profile form. Proceed to sum each column. Then plot the sums and obtain percentiles and *T* scores.

The ninth scale, *Sex Problems,* does not contribute to a composite. To obtain this score, if desired, sum the scores for items 5, 59, 60, 73, 96, and 110. Table 4.6 provides a *T* score for each raw score. The Sex Problems scale is found only on the CBCL/4-18, and only for ages 4–11 years.

Composites and Total Problems Score

The CBCL/4-18 provides eight total scores, and the CBCL/2-3 provides six. Examiners can quickly calculate an optional ninth scale and can obtain *Inter-*

Table 4.6 Raw Scores and *T* Scores for the CBCL Sex Problems Scale

Boys		Girls	
Raw Score	*T* Score	Raw Score	*T* Score
0	50	0	50
1	65	1	64
2	70	2	70
3	73	3	73
4	76	4	76
5	79	5	79
6	82	6	82
7	85	7	85
8	88	8	88
9	91	9	91
10	94	10	94
11	97	11	97
12	100	12	100

Source: Achenbach (1991a).

nalizing and *Externalizing* composite scores using easy addition and subtraction.

To obtain the overall score, simply sum all *1*s and *2*s on the CBCL. Use the protocol rather than the profile form because some items are listed on both scales. For both age groups, the box on the far right shows the *T* score corresponding to the total score.

INTERPRETING THE CHILD BEHAVIOR CHECKLIST

Interpretation of the CBCL requires a knowledge and understanding of the *Empirically Based Taxonomy: How to Use Syndromes and Profile Types Derived From the CBCL/4-18, TRF, and YSR* (Achenbach, 1993). This volume requires a great deal of study and background; much of it can be omitted for purposes of interpretation. The manual (Achenbach, 1991a) also provides a brief summary of scale interpretation. Each CBCL scale may be interpreted in terms of the construct being measured. A high score on the Aggressive Behavior scale, for example, would indicate a high degree of aggression.

Item Examination

The information obtained in this way is fairly rudimentary. We suggest that practitioners supplement this approach by taking individual items into account. A scale label such as *Aggressive Behavior* is always someone's interpretation and is based on groups rather than individuals. Therefore, such a label is an imperfect summary of the underlying symptoms it is meant to describe; it may be more or less suited to an individual examinee. In addition, a consideration of the items themselves provides for richer, more detailed interpretation than does the scale label alone. Finally, the items can reveal information that the scale label does not suggest.

The Anxious/Depressed scale is an apt example. A young person may endorse primarily such items as:

12. *Complains of loneliness*
14. *Cries a lot*
33. *Feels or complains that no one loves him/her*
35. *Feels worthless or inferior*
52. *Feels too guilty*
103. *Is unhappy, sad, or depressed*
112. *Worries*

The examinee could obtain a score in the borderline or even the clinical range. These items would suggest depressive symptoms. By contrast, a mixture of these items with the following

31. *Fears he/she might do something bad*
32. *Feels he/she has to be perfect*
45. *Is nervous, high-strung, or tense*
50. *Is too fearful or anxious*

would suggest the additional presence of anxiety.

Thus, an item examination can provide information about what a scale score means for a particular examinee. A high Anxious/Depressed score may point rather directly to depression or may indicate a larger span of symptoms that also includes anxiety. Beyond this, children who have about the same mix of anxious versus depressed symptoms can differ among themselves. A child who complains of loneliness and who feels unloved and inferior is expressing difficulties quite different from a child who is *self-conscious or easily embarrassed* (item 71), *feels too guilty* (item 52), is *too fearful or anxious* (item 50), and *feels others are out to get him/her* (item 34). Follow-up will be different for the two children. Thus, an item examination can clarify the overall scale label, which describes some examinees better than others; can greatly enrich the interpretation suggested by a scale score; and can provide additional information not suggested by the scale score.

Poorly Performing Items

In Heubeck's (2000) research, the items responsible for the relatively poor findings for Achenbach's (1991a) model were items 1, 45, 55, 56e, 62, 63, 75, 80, 93, 101, 103, and 105. These troublesome items included all five of those placed on two or three scales: 1, 45, 62, 80, and 103. Although these items were weak, other items improved the fit of Achenbach's (1991a) model when included in more than one scale. Overall, the CBCL proved to be sound. A large majority (90%) of the items correlated with the appropriate factors (Heubeck, 2000).

Relative Support for Attention Problems and Other Scales

The best-supported CBCL scales, as reported by Heubeck (2000), were Withdrawn, Somatic Problems, Anxious/Depressed, Thought Problems, and Aggressive Behavior. Heubeck found least support for the Attention Problems scale in the three countries studied or reported: Holland, Australia, and the United States. Heubeck noted that "9 out of 14 items supposed to measure attention problems demonstrated low loadings on one or the other model" (p. 445–446). Rather than address these items per se, Heubeck called attention to the items that remained strong in different cultures: item 8, *Can't concentrate, can't pay attention for long;* item 10, *Can't sit still, restless, or hyperactive;* and item 41, *Impulsive or acts without thinking.*

A larger number of items very likely showed higher loadings in one or two countries. Nonetheless, we suggest supplementing the CBCL Attention Problems scale with an attention scale from one or more other inventories and relying primarily on this latter scale. If ADHD is the chief concern for a child or adolescent, the examiner should consider an alternative test with well-supported attention and related scales.

Interpretive Indications From Heubeck

Specific Syndrome Scales

Aggressive Behavior. Heubeck (2000) argued that the Aggressive Behavior scale should be redefined as "Emotional Acting Out." *Crying, sulking,* and *showing no guilt* were highly correlating items that lead to this new label. We suggest that examiners consider this descriptor for individual examinees to determine if it might best describe them.

Delinquent Behavior. Heubeck (2000) suggested a redefinition of this scale as "Covert Antisocial Behavior." The actual difference in item content appeared small, but the absence of demonstrative antisocial behaviors, such as fighting, attacking, and threatening, indicated that this redefinition should be considered when interpreting the scale. By contrast, several demonstrative antisocial behaviors, such as those noted just above, were closely associated with the Aggressive Behavior factor.

Attention Problems. With children and adolescents, the Attention Problems subscale appears to perform best at T scores of 60 (e.g., Biederman et al., 1993; Steingard, Biederman, Doyle, & Sprich-Buckminster, 1992; Eiraldi et al., 2000). Doyle et al. (1997) reported a somewhat different finding with a school sample when testing for ADHD. The best results occurred at a T score of 65 for discrimination between ADHD and non-ADHD children and adolescents, as assessed with a parent-structured interview.

Social Problems. Heubeck (2000) reported that this scale changed markedly in confirmatory factor analyses (CFAs). Items newly correlating with the scale included *attacks, fights, is mean, threatens,* and *does not get along with others.* Several of these items had violent content. Heubeck argued for a major redefinition of the scale, naming it "Mean Aggression With Associated Social Problems." Here, the model of DeGroot et al. (1994) fared better than that of Achenbach (1991a).

According to Heubeck (2000), the original scale definition portrays "an immature and clumsy child who does not get along with peers." The redefined factor portrays "a child who may be rejected, but who is mean, destructive, antisocial, and probably a bully" (p. 446). Practitioners should consider this new conceptualization when interpreting scores for individual examinees. Children with rejected status (as opposed to ignored status) tend to be aggressive and intrusive. This scale is potentially important because people who are measured as having rejected sociometric status as children have more serious difficulties later in life. The connection with sociometrics may not be established, but the potential for relevance is substantial.

Composites

Heubeck (2000) suggested a reinterpretation of the CBCL as incorporating three factors, which might be labeled as emotional acting out, mean and destructive aggression, and evasive delinquency. For the first two factors, Heubeck has clearly made a good case. Evasive delinquency has at least suggestive support, and examiners might consider it when interpreting profiles.

ADMINISTERING THE TEACHER RATING FORM

Initial Considerations

As with the previous chapter, material is presented for the TRF only when it diverges from the already presented CBCL. The TRF comes with a scannable version and a hand-scored version. In addition to the TRS for examinees aged 5–18 years, the C-TRF covers ages 2–5; a teacher or another caregiver may complete this inventory. The instructions are clear enough so that most respondents should have little or no difficulty completing either form. Finally, the person presenting either inventory is called upon to answer any questions the respondent may have (Achenbach, 1991b, 1997a).

In some school systems, teachers use the TRF routinely when initiating referrals. Copies of the inventory are available for all children or adolescents that a teacher wishes to refer. Nonetheless, a professional trained in psychological assessment should use the completed TRF form. As with any test, the results should be available only to authorized individuals—for instance, a school psychologist (Achenbach, 1991b).

According to Achenbach and Edelbrock (1983), the TRF is a "counterpart of the CBCL for rating school behavior" (p. 132). To those administering the TRF, they suggest administering the CBCL also to obtain directly comparable information. In addition, examiners can administer additional protocols to additional teachers.

Rapport and Instructions

The instructions for the TRF are very similar to those for the CBCL. Only a few additional remarks are needed here. The TRF protocol should be self-administered by a teacher who has known the student for at least 2 months. The protocol requires about 10 minutes to complete but may take longer for teachers who add extensive comments and many scores from achievement, readiness, and aptitude tests (Achenbach, 1991b).

As Achenbach (1991b) notes, teachers are asked to complete numerous forms for which they receive insufficient explanations. To facilitate rapport, then, a clinician or other professional familiar with the TRF should show it to the teacher in advance, explaining its purpose and remaining available to answer any questions the teacher may have. Similarly, anyone from outside the school system requesting completion of the TRS should explain the reason for the request through a personal contact or letter, provide a consent form signed by a parent or other responsible party, and be available to answer any questions.

Explanations of the TRS should stress the importance of the teacher's expertise and knowledge of the student. Such an appeal to the teacher's professionalism enhances rapport. Examiners should avoid communicating with teachers as if they were professionals addressing laypeople or as if their knowledge exceeded that of teachers.

SCORING THE TEACHER RATING FORM

Items I through IX

Of these initial items, score only VII and VIII. For item VII, Current School Performance, the teacher lists current academic subjects and rates the student's performance in each subject. The ratings range from 1 *(far below grade)* to 5 *(far above grade)*.

To score item VII, find the mean of the *academic* subjects listed. Enter this mean under Academic Performance on the reverse side of the profile. If a teacher has checked two boxes for one subject, find the mean of the two scores. Use this mean as the score for that subject when you obtain the mean for the entire item.

To oversimplify somewhat, a standardized test is one that is the same for all examinees. For open-ended items, test developers may provide guidelines for all examiners in order to increase the items' standardization. For item VII of the TRS, Achenbach (1991b) has provided guidelines as to which subjects should be treated as academic ones (see Rapid Reference 4.2).

Item VIII consists of questions. For each question, the teacher assigns a rating from 1 *(much less)* to 7 *(much more)*. Enter each rating under the appropriate heading on the profile: *working hard, behaving appropriately, learning,* or *happy*. Next, add the four ratings and enter the sum in the next column. Do not add the ratings if one is missing.

The Problem Scales

The caveats noted for the CBCL problem scales also apply to the TRF. For example, clinicians should score a particular problem on only one item. If a prob-

⚏Rapid Reference 4.2

....

Guidelines for Item VII of the Teacher's Report Form

Examples of Academic Subjects

Reading	Foreign Language
Writing	Science
Arithmetic	History
Spelling	Social Studies
English	

Examples of Nonacademic Subjects

Art	Driver Education
Music	Industrial Arts
Typing	Home Economics
Physical Education	

Source: Achenbach (1991b).

lem specified by a closed-ended item appears also as an open-ended response, score only the closed-ended item. For example, if a teacher has written "can't sit still" or anything entirely covered by item 10, score only item 10. Under item 56d, *problems with eyes,* enter 0 for problems with an organic basis, such as "wears glasses" or "farsighted" (Achenbach, 1991b).

INTERPRETING THE TEACHER RATING FORM

As with the CBCL, little clear interpretive information is available for the TRF, particularly for its subscales. The indications for the CBCL are generally relevant to the TRF. Each scale may be interpreted in terms of the construct being measured. An item examination can add rich information to this basic interpretation. In addition, research results for the CBCL (e.g., Heubeck, 2000) may be considered for the TRF, given the consistency provided by the cross-informant syndromes.

ADMINISTERING THE YOUTH SELF-REPORT

Initial Considerations

As with the previous chapter, material is presented for the YSR only when it diverges from previous information. The YSR covers children and adolescents aged 11–18 years. Young people completing the YSR should have both a mental age of at least 10 years and at least fifth-grade reading skills.

Rapport and Instructions

Regarding the instructions, the YSR is similar to the TRF and CBCL. Only a few additional remarks are needed here. The protocol takes about 15 minutes to complete, but administration can take longer for children who give lengthy responses to the open-ended items (Achenbach, 1991c). The instructions may be somewhat advanced for some students.

Someone familiar with the YSR should tell the child in language appropriate to the child's mental age the reason for the test's administration. An example from Achenbach (1991c) is, "I would like you to fill out this form in order to obtain your views of your interests, feelings, and behavior" (p. 12). Like the CBCL, the YSR may be administered orally to youths with poor reading skills. In a short time, these examinees may begin to complete the protocol on their own. As Achenbach suggests, oral administration should take place in a private location so that others do not overhear.

SCORING THE YOUTH SELF-REPORT

Scoring is generally the same for the YSR as for the tests covered previously in this chapter. Nonetheless, several details are different. Rapid References 4.3 and 4.4 outline these details for the Competence scales and Problem scales, re-

Rapid Reference 4.3

Youth Self-Report Scoring That Departs from That of Other Achenbach Batteries: Competence Scales

- Omit item I-A *(Number of sports)* from scoring.[a]
- If a score that contributes to the total score of the Activities Scale is missing, do not substitute the mean as you would with the CBCL. Leave the overall Activities Scale unscored.[a]
- For item VI-D, the YSR has *Do things by yourself?* The CBCL has *Play and work alone?*[b]
- The YSR has an Academic Performance scale that consists of item VII, *Mean Performance.* The CBCL instead has a School scale that consists of four items. One of them is the same as YSR *Mean Performance.*[c, d]
- Leave unscored any comments written by the young person in the areas below item VII.[b]
- Be sure to use the appropriate column headed *boys* or *girls* when entering the young person's total competence score on the profile form.

Note: The protocols, profile forms, and manuals (Achenbach, 1991a, 1991c) differ in their presentations of some items. The footnotes below indicate the sources used. All protocols and profile forms are dated 1991.

[a]YSR profile form.

[b]YSR protocol.

[c]CBCL profile form.

[d]YSR and CBCL manuals (Achenbach, 1991a, 1991c).

≡ *Rapid Reference 4.4*

....

Youth Self-Report Scoring That Departs from That of Other Achenbach Tests: Problem Scales

- Omit the Problem Scales composite from scoring if data are missing for more than eight items, excluding only items 2, 4, and 56h. The YSR omits item 113.
- If two numbers are circled for an item, score 1 for that item.
- The YSR has 103 problem items, although the last item number is 112. Items such as 4 (*I have asthma*) do not contribute to a problem scale.
- Omit the following items from scoring.

6	59	80	106
15	60	88	107
28	73	92	108
49	78	98	109

Because these items can produce inaccurate scores as a result of social desirability, they do not appear on the profile form.

- Omit from scoring any comments written by the examinee at the bottom of page 4.

spectively. In addition, guidelines for scoring five items depart from those of the tests covered previously. Rapid Reference 4.5 presents these guidelines in an abbreviated form and lists items that have the same guidelines as the CBCL.

When obtaining total raw scores for the syndrome scales, exclude the Other Problems column from scoring because these items do not form a scale. When completing the Graphic Display and computing T scores, be sure to use the correct column, designated *boys* or *girls*.

Optional scale IX is a Self-Destructive/Identity Problems scale scored only for boys. To compute the raw score for this scale, sum the 0s, 1s, and 2s for the following items:

5	18	33	79
12	20	35	91
13	27	57	110

To obtain the T score, consult Table 4.7.

≡Rapid Reference 4.5

Youth Self-Report Item Guidelines That Depart from Those of Other Achenbach Tests

Item	Content	Guideline
9	Can't get mind off certain thoughts	Score even nonobsessional responses, unless covered by another item. For age-appropriate responses such as "boys," "girls," and "cars," score as the examinee has scored them.
40, 70	Hears things, sees things	Score responses such as "ringing in ears" and "spots before eyes" as the examinee has scored them.
66	Repeats actions	Score even noncompulsive responses unless they are covered by another item.
77	Sleeps more than most people	Do not score "want to stay in bed." Do score difficulties waking up.

Item Guidelines That Do Not Depart Markedly from Those of Other Achenbach Tests

Item	Content
46	Nervous movements
56d	Problems with eyes
84	Strange behavior
85	Strange ideas
105	Alcohol or drugs

INTERPRETING THE YOUTH SELF-REPORT

Interpretation of the YSR is the same as for the tests addressed previously in this chapter. The research results presented earlier may also be considered for this measure. A clinician can interpret YSR scores in terms of the constructs measured (e.g., Anxious/Depressed, Aggressive Behavior). Item analysis can contribute considerably to this approach.

Table 4.7 Raw Scores and T Scores for YSR Scale IX, Self-Destructive/Identity Problems

Raw Score	T Score	Raw Score	T Score
0–1	50	13	79
2	53	14	81
3	58	15	83
4	61	16	85
5	64	17	87
6	66	18	89
7	68	19	91
8	70	20	93
9	72	21	94
10	74	22	96
11	76	23	98
12	78	24	100

Source: Achenbach (1991c).

USING THE PROFILE TYPES

Achenbach (1993) has identified 12 profile types that, taken together, are consistent with about half the respondents tested (see Figures 4.1–4.3). Four *cross-informant* profile types are common to the CBCL, TRF, and YSR. The remaining six profile types are unique to particular tests. Practitioners can use the 1993 editions of the computer programs for the CBCL, TRF, and YSR, as well as the cross-informant program, to generate *item-characteristic curves* (ICCs), figures that quantify how closely a young person's profile resembles the various profile types. An ICC ≥ .445, equal to a Pearson *r* of about .59, is statistically significant.

A practitioner can, however, stipulate other cutoff points to classify a child according to the profile types. The alternate cutoff point should be selected before the ICCs are known. Otherwise, the ICCs can influence the clinician and

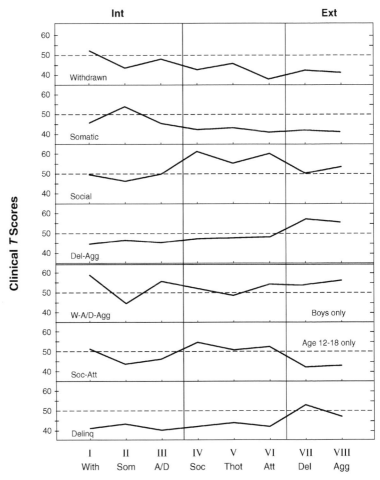

Figure 4.1 Centroids of CBCL versions of cross-informant profile types (above double line) and profile types specific to the CBCL (below double line).

Source: Achenbach (1993, p. 66). Copyright by T. M. Achenbach. Reproduced by Permission.

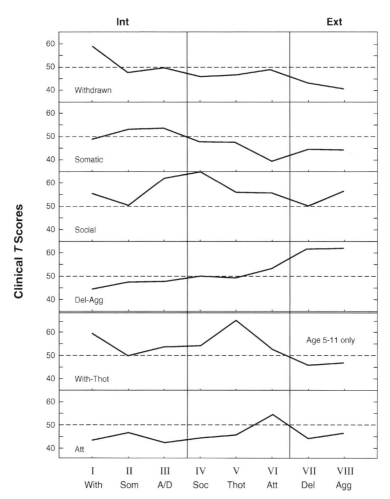

Figure 4.2 Centroids of TRF versions of cross-informant profile types (above double line) and profile types specific to the TRF (below double line).

Source: Achenbach (1993, p. 67). Copyright by T. M. Achenbach. Reproduced by Permission.

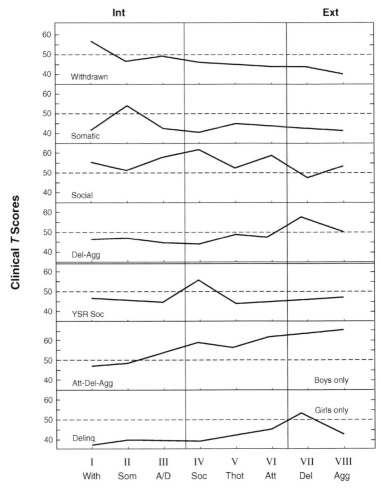

Figure 4.3 Centroids of YSR versions of cross-informant profile types (above double line) and profile types specific to the YSR (below double line).

Source: Achenbach (1993, p. 68). Copyright by T. M. Achenbach. Reproduced by Permission.

possibly alter the classification made. This is true whenever statistical significance or other cutoff points are used: Researchers and practitioners alike must
set their criteria in advance.

Profiles that are not consistent with a profile type are no less valid, informative, or interpretable than other profiles (Achenbach, 1993). In fact, people
who defy neat classification are the rule rather than the exception. In *DSM-IV*
diagnosis, for instance, the Not Otherwise Specified diagnoses are the most
frequently used. Thus, clinicians must resist the temptation to try to make a
child's profile fit a preestablished type.

🐟 TEST YOURSELF 🐟

1. **Most parents with at least _____ may complete the CBCL.**
   - (a) fifth-grade reading skills
   - (b) ninth-grade reading skills
   - (c) average measured intelligence
   - (d) low average measured intelligence

2. **The CBCL is**
   - (a) a single inventory that a child, parent, or educational professional may complete.
   - (b) a set of three tests, including child, parent, and teacher versions, for each of three age levels.
   - (c) one of several tests, among them a Young Adult Self-Report and a Caregiver-Teacher Report Form.
   - (d) a comprehensive battery for young children that assesses behavior from examinee, peer, parent, and teacher perspectives.

3. **The CBCL protocols are**
   - (a) unusually easy to administer.
   - (b) relatively easy to administer, and difficult elements typically have a purpose.
   - (c) unnecessarily hard to administer because of two pages of extraneous history items.
   - (d) extremely easy to administer but sacrifice complete coverage.

(continued)

4. Practitioners should _____ the background and history items in the first section of the CBCL/4-8.

(a) score

(b) select among

(c) typically omit

(d) qualitatively interpret

5. To score the CBCL, the examiner should place a template over the page being scored and

(a) enter the item scores in the specified squares in the computer scoring program.

(b) enter the item scores into the appropriate matrix on the item scoring form.

(c) write the item scores in the appropriate columns on the profile form.

(d) write the item scores in the formula list below the scoring table.

6. After summing the item scores, the examiner should

(a) divide by the number of subtests and obtain a percentile and T score.

(b) divide by the number of items and obtain percentiles and T scores.

(c) enter each sum in the box indicated by the arrows.

(d) plot the sums and obtain percentiles and T scores.

7. An item examination

(a) is a required procedure specified in the CBCL manual.

(b) is misleading because its reliability and validity are very low.

(c) is a subjective procedure that should be avoided when interpreting subtest scores.

(d) can take interpretive information from the group level to the level of the individual examinee.

8. Based on scientific evidence, Heubeck argued that the Social Problems scale should be

(a) redefined slightly as a Social Awkwardness measure.

(b) redefined markedly as a Mean Aggression measure.

(c) refined as to item content and perhaps redefined.

(d) defined as it is but refined as to item content.

9. **Heubeck also suggested reinterpreting the CBCL as a measure of three factors, which might be labeled**

   (a) emotional acting out; manipulative, social aggression; and sensation seeking.

   (b) emotional acting out; mean, destructive aggression; and evasive delinquency.

   (c) emotional withdrawal; diffident, social awkwardness; and arrogant, pious elitism.

   (d) emotional withdrawal; mean, destructive aggression; and manipulative, social aggression.

10. **When interpreting a child's CBCL results, practitioners must**

   (a) determine which of 12 profile types best fits the child's profile.

   (b) remember that more than 80% of all profiles studied fit a profile type.

   (c) regard any profile that does not fit a profile type as having questionable validity.

   (d) understand that many profiles do not fit a profile type but are no less valid as a result.

Answers: 1. a; 2. c; 3. b; 4. a; 5. c; 6. d; 7. d; 8. b; 9. b; 10. d

Five

CONNERS' RATING SCALES–REVISED

Conners' revised scales include separate versions for completion by parents, teachers, and adolescents. Each of the three versions is available in a long form, denoted by *L*, and a short form, denoted by *S*. Two indexes are also available separately: Conners' Global Index (CGI) in parent and teacher versions, and Conners' ADHD/*DSM-IV* Scales (CADS) in parent, teacher, and adolescent versions. Each CADS inventory has an ADHD and a *DSM-IV* Symptoms Subscales component, either of which can be administered separately, reducing the time required. Table 5.1 shows the available versions of Conners' Rating Scales–Revised (CRS-R) with administration times and numbers of items. Rapid Reference 5.1 outlines additional information about the CRS-R.

The parent and teacher versions and the auxiliary scales are appropriate for examinees aged 3–17 years. The self-report scales are appropriate for adolescents aged 12–17 years. Results for subjects a few months outside these ranges are likely to be reasonably accurate. As with any test, however, the potential for error increases with the subject's departure from the age range of the test (Conners, 1997).

The CRS-R manual provides readability statistics calculated with the Flesch reading ease formula (Flesch, 1948). Rapid Reference 5.2 shows the results for each test. For the CPRS-R:L, administrators can omit items found only on the *DSM-IV* Inattentive subscale: items 10, 20, 30, and 79. Reading ease then increases from 52.35 (grade 9) to 60.77 (grade 8). With these items excluded, however, practitioners cannot calculate the *DSM-IV* total score (Conners, 1997).

The Multi-Health Systems QuikScore format permits easy administration and scoring. Conversion from raw scores to *T* scores is automatic, and a graphic display aids in assessment and in presenting results to other parties

Table 5.1 Versions of the CRS-R with Administration Times and Numbers of Items

Version	Administration Time in Minutes	Number of Items
Long Versions		
CPRS-R:L	15–20	80
CTRS-R:L	about 15	59
CASS:L	15–20	87
Short Versions		
CPRS-R:S	5–10	27
CTRS-R:S	5–10	28
CASS:S	5–10	27
Auxiliary Scales		
CGI-P	about 5	10
CGI-T	about 5	10
CADS-P	5–10	12, 18, or 26[a]
CADS-T	5–10	12, 18, or 27[a]
CADS-A	5–10	12, 18, or 30[a]

Source: Conners (1997).

Note. CPRS-R = Conners' Parent Rating Scales–Revised; CTRS-R = Conners' Teacher Rating Scales–Revised; CASS = Conners-Wells' Adolescent Self-Report Scale; CGI = Conners' Global Index; CADS = Conners' ADHD/*DSM-IV* Scales. R = Revised, L = Long, S = Short, P = Parent, T = Teacher, A = Adolescent.

[a]The two components of these measures, ADHD Index and *DSM-IV* Symptoms Subscales, can be administered separately to reduce administration time.

such as parents and teachers. New Treatment Progress ColorPlot forms are useful for plotting treatment effects or other changes over time. Unlike the BASC ADHD Monitor series, however, the ColorPlot forms do not provide for statistical comparisons.

INITIAL CONSIDERATIONS

Whenever possible, administer CRS-R tests to all respondents: parents, teachers, and adolescents. No self-report forms are currently available for children under 12. Alternative self-reports are available for this age group (Conners,

≡ Rapid Reference 5.1

Conners' Rating Scales–Revised (CRS-R)

Author: C. Keith Conners

Publication Date: Original: 1989
Revised: 1997

What the test measures: Behavior problems.

Administration time: Regular version, up to 30 min; short forms, 5 min

Qualification of examiners: Graduate- or professional-level training in psychological assessment.

Publisher: Multi-Health Systems
P.O. Box 950
North Tonawanda, NY 14120-0950
800-456-3003
www.mhs.com

Prices: Starter set: $193.00 (as of September 2001)

≡ Rapid Reference 5.2

Readability Levels of Conners' Rating Scales–Revised

Test	Readability Score	Grade Equivalent
CPRS-R:L	52.35	9
CTRS-R:L	54.59	9
CASS:L	83.32	6
CPRS-R:S	47.85	10
CTRS-R:S	52.20	9
CASS:S	88.88	6

Note. CPRS-R = Conners' Parent Rating Scales–Revised; CTRS-R = Conners' Teacher Rating Scales–Revised; CASS = Conners-Wells' Adolescent Self-Report Scale; CGI = Conners' Global Index; CADS = Conners' ADHD/DSM-IV Scales; L = Long, S = Short.

1997), and the BASC and Achenbach self-reports have substantial empirical support.

Selecting a CRS-R Form

The current versions of the CRS-R have roughly equivalent norms, reliabilities, and validities. The long forms are preferable to the short forms because they provide more information and are more comprehensive for clinical purposes. In addition, the long forms contain numerous subscales, including the *DSM-IV* Symptoms Subscales. Conners (1997) suggests administering forms of the same length to all informants. This approach increases the comparability of results. Even the long forms, however, are less comprehensive in coverage than the BASC or the CBCL, and the 5- to 10-minute difference seems worthwhile for the additional information provided by the latter two scales.

Conners (1997) suggests that the short forms are ideal when brevity of administration is important, as with managed-care or repeated administrations. Different versions are used with different referral questions, however, so the practitioner may need to have additional CRS-R protocols completed later if the diagnosis does not fit the initial referral questions. The use of additional forms ultimately adds time and effort to the process of using the scales, easily offsetting any time saved by using the shorter forms.

The practitioner must also consider which conditions are potential concerns. Rapid Reference 5.3 lists possible uses for the CRS-R and the versions suggested for them. Practitioners should give careful thought to the form to be used with a particular client.

Appropriate Use and Qualifications for Use

The CRS-R inventories are suitable for managed-care contexts because they permit a quantifying and measuring of numerous behavioral problems, and because they are very helpful in determining whether treatment is necessary, when it is effective, and when it should be terminated. They are not appropriate, however, for informants who are disoriented, severely impaired, or un-

≡ *Rapid Reference 5.3*

··

Possible Uses of Conners' Measures

Versions or Measures	Uses or Conditions of Interest
Conners' Global Index	Hyperactivity
	Monitor general behavior change
Conners' ADHD/*DSM-IV* Scales	Clinical diagnosis
	Risk of ADHD
CPRS-R:S, CTRS-R:S, CASS:S	Conduct problems
	Cognitive problems
	Hyperactivity

Source: Conners (1997).

Note. CPRS-R = Conners' Parent Rating Scales–Revised; CTRS-R = Conners' Teacher Rating Scales–Revised; CASS = Conners-Wells' Adolescent Self-Report Scale; L = Long, S = Short.

willing to respond honestly (Conners, 1997). The CRS-R does not as yet provide validity scales to assess for such difficulties. Therefore, the inventories are largely unsuited for use in legal and forensic settings, where validity scales and other measures of dissimulation take on great importance.

For informants with limited reading or English language ability, an examiner may read the items aloud. Respondents can then record their answers using the QuikScore form or the CRS-R Computer Program (Conners, 1997). Measures of the equivalence of norms under these conditions are not available, so the effect of the change on *T* scores is unknown to practitioners. This use of the QuikScore form or the Computer Program is an application in need of scientific study.

Conners (1997) notes that untrained individuals can easily administer and score the CRS-R, but that a "mature professional" must take ultimate responsibility for its interpretation (p. 8). This person must recognize the limitations of screening and testing procedures with such instruments. Users of any test, Conners writes, must understand the basic principles and limitations of psychological testing, especially interpretation. Rapid Reference 5.4 shows re-

≡*Rapid Reference 5.4*

Requirements for Using Conners' Rating Scales–Revised

- Be familiar with the manual.
- Be familiar with the professional testing standards elaborated by the AERA, the APA, and the NCME (1999).
- Be a member of an association that endorses a set of standards for the ethical use of psychological testing, or be a licensed professional in psychology, education, medicine, social work, or a related field.
- Have postgraduate training at the master's level or beyond.

Source: Conners (1997).

Note. APA = American Psychological Association; AERA = American Educational Research Association; NCME = National Council on Measurement in Education.

quirements for using the CRS-R. Parents and others often ask questions about items and their meanings. Thus, practitioners who do use technicians or other paraprofessionals should train them in proper test administration and instruct them in how to respond to such inquiries.

ADMINISTERING THE CRS-R

Test Setting and Materials

Respondents should complete the CRS-R in one sitting if possible. The setting should be quiet and free from distractions. For the paper-and-pencil versions of the CRS-R, the only supplies needed are a profile form and soft-lead pencils, preferably without erasers. A calculator is optional. Respondents should not erase their answers on the QuikScore form because an eraser would smudge the form below. Instead, they should draw an X over any incorrect markings, then circle the correct response (Conners, 1997).

Administration Time and Other Timing Considerations

As shown in Table 5.1, the long versions of the CRS-R take about 15–20 minutes to administer, whereas the short versions take about 5–10 minutes. The

CGI requires about 5 minutes, and the CADS, 5–10 minutes. For the norming research on the CRS-R, respondents completed the protocol in a single sitting. Therefore, clinical respondents should do the same; if a single sitting is impossible, the respondent must complete the protocol within a couple of days or begin again (Conners, 1997).

The CTRS-R should be administered at least 1–2 months after the start of the school year to allow teachers time to become acquainted with the child or adolescent. In addition, the protocols call for respondents to comment on the young person's behavior over the past month. Administrators should allow for this time requirement also.

When using the CRS-R to assess effects of medication, the practitioner should obtain ratings at times when the medications are in effect. The effects of a drug administered at school, for example, may wear off by the time a child returns home. A practitioner should assess for such effects at school rather than at home (Conners, 1997).

In general, medication effects should not be assessed at times or in settings in which they tend to be unusually weak or strong, such as during a class period when a drug is characteristically at its peak performance for the client. Exceptions are possible, among them assessment planned for such settings as part of an overarching evaluation that takes place at multiple places and times. Practitioners should consider the time and setting of an administration (e.g., recess) during interpretation.

Multiple Baselines and Regression to the Mean

In assessing treatment effects, the practitioner should administer the protocol at least twice before treatment begins to avoid regression to the mean, in which people whose scores are extreme obtain more average scores at another administration (Conners, 1997; Ramsay, 1997). Conners suggests that parents and teachers usually seek treatment when behavior is at its worst, so that the first administration produces inflated results. Scores are less extreme when obtained again later.

In statistical terms, regression to the mean occurs whenever a nonrandom (systematic) sample is drawn. The mean of such a sample always differs from the population mean. When exasperated parents or teachers refer their children—for hyperactivity, for example—they create a nonrandom sample whose mean hyperactivity is higher than that of the overall population of hyperactive children.

Regression to the mean is an effect of chance. In the example above, random chance is largely responsible for the children's hyperactivity scores being unusually high at the time of referral. When the second set of scores is closer to average, chance is having less of an effect on them. So, extreme scores, if selected by exasperated parents and teachers or by some other nonrandom influence, are likely to be more moderate at a second measurement (Ramsay, 1997, 2000; Ramsay & Reynolds, 2000b). To coin a term, the *exasperation effect* to which Conners alludes is one way in which nonrandomly selected and therefore extreme scores are accidentally obtained.

By contrast, random selection results in a *representative sample,* including scores at both extremes and more moderate scores. Taken together, these scores are already average: Given sufficient sample size, their mean is equal to the population mean. Therefore, they cannot regress any farther toward this mean.

In nonrandom selection, the relatively moderate scores observed at the second administration more accurately reflect the characteristic under investigation. All else being equal, a score that has a smaller association with one characteristic has a correspondingly larger association with other characteristics, such as hyperactivity. Therefore, scores *less* strongly influenced by chance will be *more* strongly associated with the characteristic they are meant to measure—in a word, more *valid.*

Practitioners should understand that Galton's famous regression to the mean is a group phenomenon. It influences the average score of a group—referred children from a certain elementary school, for example—projecting the score upward or downward. Individual children within that group, however, will not have uniformly increased or decreased scores. One child may have an increased score; another, a decreased score; and still another, a score that remains about the same.

Thus, a practitioner may be tempted to say, "My last client got the same score at the first and second administrations. Next time, I'll dispense with multiple baselines." Unfortunately, an average of all the practitioner's clients would still show the familiar regression pattern. Thus, multiple baselines are still important—to avoid regression to the mean and for other reasons too.

We can, however, offer an encouraging word about regression. Test scores that are more reliable over time are less vulnerable to this phenomenon. Thus, a test that provides extremely high test-retest reliabilities minimizes regression to the mean. We recommend that test developers work to increase their test-retest reliabilities.

A final characteristic of regression to the mean is that it does not depend on time. Just as children who score extremely high at a first administration score closer to the mean at a second administration, children who score extremely high at a second administration will have scored closer to the mean at the first administration. An explanation of this puzzling phenomenon is beyond the scope of this book. The reversible quality of regression may seem less baffling, however, if we note that high scorers at the first and second administrations are two different groups of people. One group happens to score extremely high the first time, and the other group scores high the second time. Perhaps this brief observation can alleviate some of the perplexity that is bound to arise when an event seems almost to act backward in time.

Avoiding Potential Bias or Invalidity

Bias and invalidity are essentially the same concept. By whatever name, bias can be reduced in a number of ways during administration. Informants should provide their own responses, for example. Parents tend to consult with one another. Although understandable, this practice should be avoided. Likewise, teachers should not consult with colleagues. Adolescents, too, should complete the CRS-R protocol on their own. Administrators should not make leading remarks or give leading answers to informants' questions. Students and beginning practitioners have particular difficulty avoiding the pitfall of leading the informant. Paraprofessionals might also need to exercise special caution. If possible, the administrator should answer questions only after an informant has responded to all items.

Conners (1997) suggests a response such as the following to informants who are unsure how to respond to an item, or who have difficulty deciding between two responses: "I know it is difficult to know how to respond to some questions, but please try as best you can and choose *one* of the responses" (adapted from p. 21). In addition, the informant should respond to all items.

Look over the completed protocol to ensure that no items are left blank. If a complete protocol is impossible to obtain, score omitted items 0. Make sure that the demographic information is complete. Retain the top response sheet in case the middle sheet is unclear. Finally, encourage the informant to discuss the CRS-R after completing it. The additional discussion encourages informants to elaborate on their responses and to provide related information (Conners, 1997).

Gender and ethnic bias associated with a test itself is a separate issue that exceeds the scope of this volume. Ethnic bias in intelligence tests in particular has evoked controversy for decades among practitioners, researchers, and laypeople (Reynolds & Ramsay, in press). Kaplan and Saccuzzo (1997) and Reynolds and Ramsay (in press) provide well-written treatments of this issue.

Rapport and Ethical Considerations

Make sure the respondent is comfortable. Explain the purpose of the CRS-R. According to Conners (1997), the practitioner may need to reassure the respondent that there are no right or wrong answers, that there is no time limit, and that answers will be kept confidential. In addition, the teacher, parent, or adolescent may feel less anxious if assured that the scales are not the only source of information that will be used.

The respondent should feel reassured, too, if the administrator clarifies that responses should be based on the *past month*. If the test being administered is part of a CADS scale, ensure that the respondent knows which part or parts of the scale to complete. As the sitting concludes, take care to thank the respondent and to provide reassurance that the responses made will be used beneficially.

Finally, Conners (1997) stresses the ethical aspects of administering the CRS-R (AERA, APA, & NCME, 1999). Informed consent, avoidance of bias, and debriefing are important components of an ethical administration. Careful attention to these concerns contributes to the respondent's confidence during a sitting. Paraprofessionals who administer a CRS-R form should receive clear instructions about these ethical considerations.

SCORING THE CRS-R

To score, remove the perforated top strip, then pull the top sheet down and off. A second sheet beneath the top one shows the items in horizontal rows, with circles around the numbers the respondent has selected. To the left of these rows are four columns. Each column includes several shaded rectangles and one or more unshaded rectangles. Simply enter each number into the unshaded rectangles, sum each column, and enter the sum at the bottom of the column.

A third and final sheet is a profile form with sections labeled *Males* and *Females*. Find the appropriate section and the correct column for each scale: 1 for ages 12–14 or 2 for ages 15–17. Next, circle the numbers corresponding to the scores that you entered at the bottom of the second sheet. Using a ruler or other aid, join the circles with straight lines. To the left of the profile is a column of *T* scores. Simply convert each raw score to a *T* score by reading across to this leftmost column.

INTERPRETING THE CRS-R

Unlike many other revised rating scales, the CRS-R includes content not driven solely by items from its earlier versions. As a result, the scale is fairly reflective of current thought on childhood emotional and behavioral problems. Conversely, the test retains some of its best-supported content, such as Conners' Global Index. In addition, the scale construction procedure has led to fairly similar items within each scale, making interpretation easier. Finally, the parent and teacher versions of the scales correspond well, facilitating comparisons in a multi-informant assessment.

Because the CRS-R contains no overall indexes, interpretation takes place primarily at the subscale level. The similarity of items within each scale makes the interpretation of scale elevations easier. Nevertheless, practitioners should inspect the items that have led to any elevation. In addition, the lack of composite scores is a limitation in discerning an examinee's overall level of problems when *T* scores are elevated between 60 and 70 on multiple scales. None of the individual scales would detect a problem, but a composite score could tell the practitioner if the overall pattern of internalizing or externalizing problems was of clinical significance. Thus, the CRS-R is problematic when used with examinees presenting any of a diverse array of problems that do not fit well with the *DSM-IV* typology. This limitation is especially troublesome in applying the CRS-R series in schools, where the IDEA criteria take precedence.

Unlike some earlier versions of the CRS (e.g., CPRS-93, CTRS-28), the

CRS-R has a fairly large norming sample, even for small age ranges. Thus, interpretations based on T scores are possible for particular age groups, enhancing developmental interpretations. CRS-R interpretations are based only on students in a regular educational milieu, however, because the norming sample did not include children receiving special education services. The failure to include children representing clinical groups in proportion to their numbers in the population creates norming problems. For mathematical reasons, entirely nonclinical norm groups tend to increase the standardized scores of examinees, frequently overidentifying them as having behavior problems.

Interpretation in Alternative Contexts

The CRS-R is suitable for several uses: monitoring change, screening, and research, in addition to clinical assessment, diagnosis, and treatment planning. When monitoring change, the practitioner should develop a plan before treatment and before administering the test. This plan should include the identification of target behaviors, the number of observation periods required, the source of the ratings, and the type of treatment. Monitoring is most effective during the school year, when teacher observations can be collected. Finally, a practitioner should not overinterpret small fluctuations in responding because they may occur by chance. Occasionally, even a large change is due to chance (Conners, 1997).

In screening, little interpretation should be made, except to note whether a full-scale evaluation may be warranted. Any CRS-R subscale is useful for screening, but the CGI and the ADHD Index, a component of the ADHD/*DSM-IV* Scales, are particularly effective. A cutoff T score of 65 is most common, but others are permissible. As with any clinical test, raising the cutoff score leads to more negative findings, both true negatives and false negatives. Likewise, lowering the cutoff score leads to more positive findings—both true and false positives (Conners, 1997).

Ethical standards stipulate that research should be conducted confidentially or anonymously (AERA, APA, & NCME, 1999). In a confidential study, the investigators can identify individual respondents but pledge not to do so. In an anonymous study, the investigators cannot identify respondents. Thus, even if the researchers are subpoenaed, for instance, the participants' identities are secure.

A researcher unexpectedly may find results indicating that a particular respondent requires additional evaluation. Here, Conners (1997) suggests treating the test as a screening instrument, forwarding the results to an appropriate person, such as a parent or school psychologist, so that appropriate intervention can occur. Finally, Conners notes that informed consent and debriefing apply as much to research as to clinical and screening procedures.

The Validity of CRS-R Responses

In the clinical use of the CRS-R, practitioners should keep certain validity considerations in mind. When two or more respondents agree as to the presence or absence of a problem, the responses of these *multiple raters* increase validity. If respondents do not agree, evaluate the ratings to determine the probable reason. A threat to validity may be to blame. One form may have been completed incorrectly or may have less validity than the others. Alternatively, one respondent may be denying or failing to recognize the existence of a problem (Conners, 1997). Other sources of information, such as direct classroom observation or interviews with a relative of the young person, may help to resolve the inconsistency.

Disagreement between respondents does not always signal invalidity. The problem may be present in some situations or settings but not others. If so, the practitioner may be able to rule out a particular *DSM-IV* diagnosis (Conners, 1997). In addition, the difference in situations or settings can be a starting point in identifying stimuli that may be eliciting the problem behavior.

Conners' Basic Interpretive Strategy

Conners (1999) outlines an approach to interpretation that is as appropriate to most other personality tests as to the CRS-R. An understanding of T scores and percentiles is central to this approach. Conners notes that T scores allow a practitioner to compare scores on different characteristics or other dimensions. For example, one examinee's T score can be compared with those of other examinees of the same gender and age range. In addition, an examinee's T score on one dimension, such as Anxiety, can be compared to the same examinee's T score on another dimension, such as Depression. These comparisons can be made without regard to the factor composition of the dimensions or to the number of items used to measure those dimensions (Conners, 1997, 1999). In other words, comparisons between T scores *control* for factor composition and number of items. This is not true of raw scores, so such comparisons between raw scores would be impossible.

When gender and age are taken into account, the CRS-R provides scores that have about the same meaning for examinees of various ethnicities. Many other personality tests, including the BASC and the Achenbach tests, have produced the same result, except that SES is also taken into account. Thus, a Hispanic examinee and an African American examinee who have the same Aggression score are about equally aggressive in their behavior if we assume that their age, gender, and SES are the same. Of considerable importance, SES has a larger role than either age or ethnicity in numerous studies with a great variety of methodologies. Associations with ethnicity frequently turn out to be chimeras when analyzed along with SES. Thus, when ethnicity becomes an issue with an examinee, it is important to consider whether SES might be a better explanation.

The most important component of Conners' Basic Interpretive Strategy is a Step-by-Step Interpretation Sequence that helps simplify the complex interpretive process. The eight steps of this sequence are summarized below (Conners, 1997, 1999).

Conners' Step-by-Step Interpretation Sequence

1. Examine Threats to Validity
For the CTRS-R, investigate whether the respondent knows the child well enough to provide for valid interpretations. For all scales, consider whether the items on the scale are appropriate for the decision being made. Other possible sources of invalidity include insensitivity to the young person's gender or cultural background, conflicts between the teacher and parent, and strained relationships between the parent and child (Conners, 1997, 1999). Rapid Reference 5.5 describes additional sources of possible invalidity.

2. Analyze Index Scores
The CRS-R provides an ADHD Index and Conners' Global Index (CGI). The first of these is available on all CRS-R forms and on the CADS. This index assesses for risk of ADHD and, if other scales such as the Hyperactivity scale are

≡ Rapid Reference 5.5

Sources of Possible Invalidity

Random Responses

Types of random responding include zigzag patterns and long strings of a single response, such as *pretty much true*. Random responding tends to flatten a profile, making an examinee's subtest scores appear more consistent than they otherwise would. Thus, differences between scores, which are central to interpretation, are concealed. A young person may respond randomly as a result of reading difficulties, low motivation, time limits that lead to rushed responding, or a misunderstanding of how the instrument will be used.

Response Bias

Respondents may portray a young person more positively or negatively than is warranted. An adolescent, for example, may try to justify disruptive behavior or relieve pressure to make good grades. Parents may want to avoid labeling or, conversely, to obtain special services for their child. Teachers may want a child removed from their classroom. Response bias distorts an examinee's scores in a particular direction, either upward or downward. The direction tends to be the same for all subscales, so differences between scales may be concealed, impeding diagnosis and interpretation. As Conners (1999) notes, the norming sample for the CRS-R responded under conditions of anonymity. Because clinical examinees are not anonymous, social desirability effects may be increased.

Inconsistent Responses

An informant's responses may conflict with each other or conflict sharply with another informant's responses. The responses may nevertheless be valid, reflecting true differences between the perceptions of different informants. For example, inconsistency may occur because a problem manifests itself in one setting but not in another. Invalidity, however, is frequently the explanation. One or both sets of responses may be misleading. A teacher, for example, may compare an examinee to other children at the same grade level, whereas a parent may use his or her childhood behavior as the standard of comparison.

Source: Adapted in part from Conners (1997, 1999).

elevated, the presence of an attentional problem (Conners, 1997). For any CRS-R inventory, the ADHD Index is "the best initial indicator" (Conners, 1999, p. 474) of an attentional or hyperactive-impulsive problem.

The second index, the CGI, was originally named the Hyperactivity Index. This 10-item scale, designed to be sensitive to treatment effects, is available on the long and short versions of both the CPRS-R and the CTRS-R. Attention problems elevate this index, but so do other forms of pathology and behavioral problems. An elevation of the CGI, perhaps accompanied by the ADHD Index, suggests internalizing problems and a considerable restless-impulsive involvement (Conners, 1997, 1999).

Results reported by Parker, Sitarenios, and Conners (1996; cited in Conners, 1997) indicate that the CGI reflects two dimensions: Restless-Impulsive and Emotional Lability. Most of the Restless-Impulsive item content is related to hyperactivity, but some involves inattentiveness. The Emotional Lability item content is related both to mood swings and to marked emotional reactions such as temper outbursts and frequent crying.

3. Examine the Overall Profile and Subscale Patterns
Practitioners should look for areas of relative strength and weakness to identify specific problem areas. Conners (1997) suggests checking for a minimum of four basic profile patterns (see Rapid Reference 5.6). In addition, Conners posits specific combinations of scale elevations that in themselves may warrant clinical attention (Rapid Reference 5.7).

4. Examine Subscale Scores
Rapid Reference 5.8 shows labels and descriptions of CASS scales; Rapid Reference 5.9 provides the same information for the CPRS-R and CTRS-R scales. Interpretations may refer either to descriptions or to labels. A practitioner may also interpret results according to the content of the items endorsed. Whatever approach is taken should follow from an item examination.

5. Analyze the DSM-IV Symptoms Subscales
At this point, your results may suggest attentional difficulties. If so, an examination of the *DSM-IV* subscales can indicate the problem's severity, and its subtype: Hyperactive-Impulsive or Inattentive. These subscales are available on the CASS:L, CPRS-R:L, CTRS-R:L, CADS-T, CADS-P, and CADS-A. If these scales are elevated, the young person would probably receive a diagnosis if the *DSM-IV* were consulted. Similarly, if 6 or more of the items are rated 3, the youth would again be likely to receive a *DSM-IV* diagnosis. As noted by Conners (1997), either result requires corroboration from a full clinical investigation.

The criterion of 3, referred to above, is a conservative one that underiden-

≡ *Rapid Reference 5.6*

....

Conners' Four Basic Profile Patterns

1. *Typical Profile.* All *T* scores are 50 or less, a healthy profile.[a]

2. *Mildly Elevated Profile.* No *T* scores exceed 65, and no more than one exceeds 60. At least one *T* score, however, is within a few points of 60—high enough to warrant concern. If other findings are also present, further testing or closer monitoring may be advisable.

3. *Elevated Profile, Type G. T* scores on three or more conceptually unrelated scales exceed 60 or 65. This profile indicates problematic functioning, either of a global character or in the form of substantial comorbidity. If the elevated scales are conceptually related, however, then problematic global functioning or comorbidity may not be present. An example of the latter, provided by Conners (1997), is an elevated Hyperactivity scale, ADHD index, and *DSM-IV* Hyperactive-Impulsive scale.

4. *Elevated Profile, Type P.* One or two scales are highly elevated, whereas the remaining scales are much lower or even average. This profile type indicates problematic functioning concentrated in specific areas. Certain patterns, such as elevated Hyperactivity, Inattention, and ADHD Index scores in the absence of other elevations, are consistent with ADHD free from comorbidity (Conners, 1999, p. 474). In contrast, the same three elevations accompanied by an elevated Oppositional score suggest the commonly found comorbidity with oppositional problems. An elevation of the ADHD Index and a high elevation of the Cognitive/Inattention subscale suggest comorbid learning disorders.

A hybrid of Type G and Type P profiles can occur when three or more subscales are high, but one or two of them are at least 5 points lower than the others. Practitioners may interpret this profile as Type P when this approach is suggested by other clinical information, or by the practitioner's judgment that treatment focused on one or two areas would be most effective.

Source: Adapted in part from Conners (1997).

[a]Conners (1999); the description in the manual (Conners, 1997) is somewhat different.

tifies young people likely to receive a *DSM-IV* diagnosis. The widespread problem of overidentification, however, is avoided. Practitioners have the option of selecting 2 rather than 3 as a criterion. This alternative results in greater identification, which sometimes is necessary to avoid excluding a child or adolescent from needed services. Conners (1997) recommends the conservative

≡ Rapid Reference 5.7

Combined Scale Elevations on the CRS-R and Possible Interpretations

Scale Combination	Possible Interpretation
Hyperactivity and *DSM-IV* Symptoms	Attention deficits with no comorbidity
Hyperactivity, *DSM-IV* Symptoms, and Oppositional	ADHD comorbid with Oppositional Defiant Disorder or Conduct Disorder
Hyperactivity, *DSM-IV* Symptoms, and Anxious-Shy	ADHD comorbid with an anxiety disorder of some type

Source: Conners (1997).

Note. CRS-R = Conners' Rating Scales–Revised.

criterion but notes that a practitioner should consider how different *DSM-IV* scores can be, depending on the criterion used.

6. Examine Item Responses

Conners (1999) suggests that interpretations at the item level serve best as hypotheses for further investigation. Responses to individual items can be informative regardless of whether the scale on which they appear shows an elevation (Conners, 1997). On the CTRS-R, for example, children whose Anxious-Shy scores are elevated may be easily hurt, emotional, and given to frequent crying (items 5, 14, and 25), or they may be primarily timid and shy (items 23 and 51). Even if no subscales are elevated, an endorsement of item 7, *Temper outbursts; explosive, unpredictable behavior,* may in itself warrant additional investigation. As Conners (1999) notes, many difficulties do not qualify as diagnosable disorders but are nevertheless important and treatable.

7. Integrate Results with All Other Available Information

Test scores alone are not enough to provide for a satisfactory assessment or treatment plan. Even a battery of personality, ability, aptitude, achievement, and neuropsychological tests is never a substitute for family interviews, class-

Labels and Descriptions of CASS Scales

Label	Description
Family Problems	High scorers are likely to perceive their parents and other family members as uncaring, harsh, or overly critical; they may also feel detached from family members.
Emotional Problems	High scorers are likely to have low self-esteem and little self-confidence, to feel lonely and isolated, and generally to have more worries and concerns than most individuals their age.
Conduct Problems	Individuals scoring high on this subscale are more likely to break rules, to have problems with persons in authority, and to be engaged in antisocial activities than other individuals their age. Many items of this subscale pertain to serious misbehavior (e.g., destruction of property, taking drugs).
Cognitive Problems / Inattention	High scorers may be inattentive. They may have more academic difficulties than most individuals their age, have problems organizing and completing tasks, and have particular trouble concentrating on work that requires mental effort.
Anger Control Problems	High scorers are more emotionally labile than most individuals their age and are easily angered and irritated by people around them.
Hyperactivity	High scorers have difficulty sitting still and feel more restless and active than most individuals their age.

Source: Conners (1997).

Note. CASS = Conners-Wells' Adolescent Self-Report Scale.

room observations, medical records, a thorough developmental history, and any other information the practitioner needs to respond credibly to the concerns that led to the evaluation. Conners (1999) and Weiss and Hechtman (1993; cited in Conners, 1997) suggest that the following information should be obtained during the course of a comprehensive assessment.

≡*Rapid Reference 5.9*

Labels and Descriptions of CPRS-R and CTRS-R Scales

Label	Description
Oppositional	Individuals scoring high on this subscale are likely to break rules, have problems with people in authority, and are more easily annoyed and angered than most individuals their age.
Cognitive Problems / Inattention	High scorers may be inattentive. They may have more academic difficulties than most individuals their age, have problems organizing their work, have difficulty completing tasks or schoolwork, and appear to have trouble concentrating on tasks that require sustained mental effort.
Hyperactivity	High scorers have difficulty sitting still, feel more restless and impulsive than most individuals their age, and have the need to be always active.
Anxious / Shy	High scorers generally have more worries and fears than most individuals their age; they are prone to be emotional, are very sensitive to criticism, are particularly anxious in new or unfamiliar situations, and appear to be very shy and withdrawn.
Perfectionism	High scorers are likely to set high goals for themselves, are very fastidious about the way they do things at home or at school, and may be more obsessive about their work or tasks than most individuals their age.
Social Problems	High scorers are likely to perceive that they have few friends, are likely to have low self-esteem and little self-confidence, and often feel more socially detached from their peers than most individuals their age.
Psychosomatic (only on CPRS-R)	High scorers report more physical symptoms (e.g., aches and pains) than most children or adolescents their age.

Source: Conners (1997).

Note. CPRS-R = Conners' Parent Rating Scales–Revised; CTRS-R = Conners' Teacher Rating Scales–Revised.

- A history of pregnancy, delivery, and developmental milestones from infancy to the present
- Information about early temperament
- A family history of medical and psychiatric disorders—severity, frequency, duration, and situational specificity
- An educational assessment, including both academic functioning and classroom behavior
- Child and family interaction patterns and family structure
- Intrapsychic processes, including self-image and sense of efficacy with family, peers, and schoolmates
- Neurological status, when indicated by other evidence

The CRS-R series does not provide for the collection of such data directly. The BASC SDH and SOS may be useful adjuncts for practitioners who prefer the CRS-R as their measure of behavior.

8. Determine the Appropriate Intervention or Strategy for Remediation

After the seventh step is completed, many kinds of test results and other information are available. Weighing ethical standards and individual circumstances, the practitioner should provide suitable feedback to the parent, to the teacher, and to the adolescent if appropriate. Practitioners need to decide who will have access to the clinical report and phrase the report accordingly. They should consider all sources of information in the development of an intervention or plan for treatment.

An appropriate alternative to treatment is to make a referral if, for example, objectivity is judged to be problematic or if the necessary treatment exceeds the practitioner's expertise. Any treatment should incorporate baseline measures and periodic, formal assessment to monitor the child's response to treatment and determine whether to modify, add, or terminate treatments (Conners, 1997; for additional information on treatment planning with the CRS-R, see Conners, 1999).

 **TEST YOURSELF**

1. **For the CRS-R parent, teacher, and adolescent inventories, _____ are available.**

    (a) clinical and nonclinical norms

    (b) long and short forms

    (c) screening and managed-care versions

    (d) composite and omnibus scores

2. **Two CRS-R indexes, called _____, are available separately.**

    (a) Conners' Global Index and Conners' ADHD/DSM-IV Scales

    (b) Conners' General Inventory and Conners' Brief ADHD Scales

    (c) Conners' Hyperactivity Scales and Conners' Attention Survey

    (d) Conners' Inattention Scales and Conners' Inactivity Index

3. **The CGI takes _____ minutes to administer; the ADHD scales take _____ minutes.**

    (a) 15 to 20; 20 to 25

    (b) 10 to 15; 10 to 20

    (c) 10; 10 to 20

    (d) 5; 5 to 10

4. **When using the CRS-R to assess effects of medication, the practitioner should obtain ratings**

    (a) after these effects have worn off.

    (b) at a time of day when these effects are at their peak.

    (c) before these effects have worn off.

    (d) just after the medication is administered.

5. **Regression to the mean occurs**

    (a) with individuals, by chance, and when an exasperation effect is present.

    (b) with groups, by chance, and when a sample is selected nonrandomly.

    (c) with individuals, over time, and when a sample is selected randomly.

    (d) with groups, over time, and when an exasperation effect is absent.

6. **To score the CRS-R, remove the top sheet of the profile. On the second sheet, you will find**

    (a) the item scores circled.

    (b) the subtest scores circled.

    (c) a set of simple formulas.

    (d) a list of brief procedures.

(continued)

7. Next, write the circled numbers in the columns on the left, sum each column, and

(a) look for the corresponding *T* score in the columns on the right.

(b) check for the corresponding percentile in the rows across the top.

(c) remove the middle sheet and enter the sum on the next page.

(d) enter the sum obtained at the bottom of the column.

8. For the CRS-R, interpretation takes place primarily at the _____ level.

(a) composite

(b) overall composite

(c) subscale

(d) individual item

9. Conners' Step-by-Step Interpretation Sequence begins with which of the following steps?

(a) Review responses for completeness, analyze index scores, and examine the overall profile and subscale patterns.

(b) Examine threats to validity, analyze index scores, and examine the overall profile and subscale patterns.

(c) Analyze clinical scores, analyze nonclinical scores, and examine the overall composite.

(d) Complete the validity checklist, analyze the three composites, and examine the overall composite.

10. The Interpretation Sequence also includes which of these steps?

(a) Analyze the CGI, review the profile plot, and examine item responses.

(b) Analyze the CGI, examine item responses, and investigate items left blank.

(c) Review open-ended items, review closed-ended items, and investigate unscored items.

(d) Analyze *DSM-IV* Symptoms Subscales, examine item responses, and integrate results with other information.

11. The Interpretation Sequence concludes with which important step?

(a) Determine if referral is needed.

(b) Summon the child's homeroom teacher.

(c) Establish clinical diagnoses or select clinical descriptors.

(d) Determine the appropriate intervention or strategy for remediation.

Answers: 1. b; 2. a; 3. d; 4. c; 5. b; 6. a; 7. d; 8. c; 9. b; 10. d; 11. d

Six

CLASSROOM OBSERVATIONS

Because classroom-based observational assessment is essential for the evaluation of school-age children, every clinician should have at least one tool for this purpose. These direct observational techniques are in widespread use today. Kamphaus and Frick (1996, p. 184) posit "two primary reasons for this infatuation with direct observations." They note first that "as the term *direct* implies, observations of behavior are not filtered through the perceptions of some informant. Instead, the behaviors of the child are observed directly." The authors explain further that numerous "variables and biases" can influence information reported by the child or by others in the child's environment. The assessors' need to account for these influences in their interpretations increases the complexity of those interpretations. "Therefore," the authors conclude, "direct observations of behavior eliminate some of the complexity in the interpretive process."

Kamphaus and Frick (1996, p. 184) also suggest a second reason for the popularity of classroom observations. Frequently, these procedures allow the examiner to assess "environmental contingencies that are operating to produce, maintain, or exacerbate a child's behavior." The authors note that direct observations can "assess how others respond to a child's behavior" or, conversely, can "detect environmental stimuli that seem to elicit certain behaviors." Finally, the authors point out that "by placing the behavior in a contextual framework, behavioral observations often lead to very effective environmental interventions."

Despite their widespread popularity, classroom observations have noteworthy limitations as well. First, one simply cannot obtain an in-depth, long-term understanding of a child's classroom behavior through observations. Whether clinicians observe for 1 hour or 10, they will not have the same lengthy sample of behavior that is available to the child's teacher. In fact, teachers' extensive knowledge of their students has contributed to the popularity and utility of teacher ratings.

DON'T FORGET

....

The presence of outside observers always has effects on the student being observed, the classroom interactions of all students, and their interactions with the teacher.

Second, the presence of an observer has a known and substantial effect on classroom behavior (Kamphaus & Frick, 2002). In other words, children display *reactivity* when an observer is present. As is noted later in this chapter, observers can take steps to minimize reactivity at least to an extent. Regardless, the reactive nature of children's behavior may prejudice the observation in unknown ways and contribute to a lack of validity.

Third, useful observations can be difficult to schedule. If, for example, a child is referred for hitting others, this relatively infrequent behavior may be difficult to observe firsthand. Another example of the difficulties involved in observing at the opportune time is child behavior that varies throughout the day. Highly variable behavior requires more time than may be feasible for an accurate representation.

Fourth, determining the behaviors to observe for an individual child may be difficult. Teachers, parents, or other referral sources sometimes have conflicting and inaccurate opinions regarding the behaviors that are problematic. Thus, an observer might arrive to observe aggressive behavior and discover that the child actually displays more problematic hyperactivity. The process of branching to ensure that all important misbehavior and adaptive behavior is assessed is difficult without a specific algorithm for doing so. In other words, the initial target behaviors for observation may not be the most important ones.

Of course, not all of these limitations can be countered using any single observation approach. We seek, however, to give observers a strategy for addressing some of these limitations, at least partially, using existing practical observation procedures.

With hundreds of procedures from which to choose, we must limit our discussion of observational procedures. We choose to emphasize the unique, comprehensive, and widely used Student Observation System (SOS) of the BASC. The SOS is applicable from preschool through high-school ages. It is useful in any structured setting but is best used in a classroom. Interested readers can access numerous other treatises on observational methods (e.g., Shapiro & Kratochwill, 2000).

We know of two principal techniques for observing classroom behavior (Rapid Reference 6.1). One technique, most often called *event recording*, is both informal and ubiquitous. With this technique, a school-based clinician observes a target child for a limited range of behaviors (e.g., hyperactivity) that a teacher or other referral source has

identified a priori. The observer then merely records the frequency of selected events (e.g., *standing on desk*). This procedure works well when the behavior to be observed is well-defined (e.g., not *worry*), is frequently displayed (e.g., not *incontinence*), and has a discrete beginning and ending (e.g., not *daydreaming*).

The other general category of commonly used observation techniques involves some form of *time sampling*. Typically, a clinician observes a child's behavior at a specified time point (e.g., every 10 seconds) and records only the behavior seen at that time. This procedure is particularly useful for behaviors of greater duration. Unfortunately, such precise timing is often difficult to carry out in the classroom, making this approach less than practical. In addition, short time intervals may require more observer training to achieve adherence to the timing and observation schedule.

As is now apparent, difficulties are involved in both event-recording and time-sampling procedures. As a result, many school-based professionals opt for less formal observational methods when faced with these difficulties. Observation procedures in schools sometimes provide only a general impression of the child's level of hyperactivity in relation to others in the class and some anecdotes that are shared with other members of an intervention team.

THE SOS AND FUNCTIONAL BEHAVIORAL ASSESSMENT

The Student Observational System (SOS) addresses some of the limitations inherent in the use of classroom observation techniques. Specifically, the SOS is designed to make practical the use of a momentary time-sampling procedure that adequately samples the full range of a child's behavior in the classroom

Table 6.1 Behavioral Categories in Parts A and B of the Student Observation System of BASC

Category and Definition	Example of Specific Behaviors
Response to Teacher/Lesson: Appropriate academic behaviors involving teacher or class	Raises hand Waits for help on assignment
Peer Interaction: Appropriate interactions with other students	Plays with other students Converses with others in discussion
Work on School Subjects: Appropriate academic behaviors that student engages in alone	Does seatwork Works at computer
Transition Movement: Appropriate nondisruptive behaviors while moving from one activity to another	Puts on/takes off coat Gets book
Inappropriate Movement: Inappropriate motor behaviors that are unrelated to classroom work	Fidgeting in seat Passing notes
Inattention: Inattentive behaviors that are not disruptive	Doodling Looking around room
Inappropriate Vocalization: Disruptive vocal behaviors	Teasing Talking out
Somatization: Physical symptoms/complaints	Sleeping Complaining of not feeling well
Repetitive Motor Movements: Repetitive behaviors that appear to have no external reward	Finger/pencil tapping Humming/singing to oneself
Aggression: Harmful behaviors directed at another person or property	Kicking others Throwing objects at others
Self-Injurious Behavior: Severe behaviors that attempt to injure one's self	Head banging Biting self
Inappropriate Sexual Behavior: Behaviors that are explicitly sexual in nature	Touching others inappropriately Imitating sexual behavior
Bowel/Bladder Problems: Urination or defecation	Wets pants

(Reynolds & Kamphaus, 1998). The following characteristics of the SOS exemplify this effort.

- Observation of both adaptive and maladaptive behaviors (see Table 6.1)
- Multiple methods, including clinician rating, time sampling, and qualitative recording of classroom functional contingencies
- A generous time-sampling interval for recording results (27 seconds)
- Operational definitions of behaviors and time-sampling categories included in the BASC manual (Reynolds & Kamphaus, 1998)
- High interrater reliabilities for the time-sampling portion, lending confidence that independent observers are likely to observe the same trends in a child's classroom behavior (see Table 6.2)

These characteristics of the SOS have contributed to its popularity as a functional behavioral assessment tool. It is crucial, for example, to have adequate operational definitions of behaviors, which in turn contribute to good interrater reliability. Without such reliability, clinicians can never know whether their observations are unique and potentially influenced by their own biases or idiosyncratic definitions of behavior.

It is also central that observations simultaneously account for a child's adap-

Table 6.2 SOS Interobserver Reliability Estimates

Behaviors	Pearson r
Adaptive behaviors	
Response to teacher and lesson	.91
Peer interaction	.98
Work on school subjects	.98
Transition movement	.99
Problem behaviors	
Disruptive movement	.89
Inappropriate vocalization	.98
Somatization	.97
Repetitive motor movements	.97
Aggression	1.00
Inappropriate sexual behavior	.69

Source: Lett and Kamphaus (1997).

tive behavior in the classroom. Only then can a clinician recommend behaviors that should be targeted for instruction, intervention, or strengthening.

Rapid Reference 6.2 lists and briefly describes Parts A, B, and C of the BASC SOS. The three parts, as well as other BASC components, can contribute to the functional assessment of behavior from multiple perspectives.

- *Frequency.* SOS Part A includes ratings of *never observed, sometimes observed,* and *frequently observed;* SOS Part B assesses frequencies by category of behavior problem, and PRS and TRS ratings tally the frequency of behavior problems.
- *Duration.* SOS Part B includes ratings of percentage of time engaged in a particular behavior by category.
- *Intensity.* SOS Part A includes ratings of *disruptive;* SOS Part B includes ratings of frequency by category.
- *Antecedent events.* SOS Part C elicits descriptions of teacher position and behavior, along with other variables that precede student misbehavior.
- *Consequences.* SOS Part C elicits descriptions of teacher behavior, peer behavior, and other variables that follow a behavior.
- *Ecological analysis of settings.* SOS allows for observations made at different times of day and in various classroom settings; the PRS may be used for the assessment of behavior in the community and home environments.

≡Rapid Reference 6.2

The Three Parts of the BASC Student Observation System

Part A

A summary rating ranks behaviors as *never observed, sometimes observed,* or *frequently observed.*

Part B

A direct behavior count is made using the momentary time sampling method.

Part C

A qualitative observation form is used to record descriptions of (a) the teacher's approach to the classroom and (b) the environment and events that precede or follow behaviors of interest.

As is evident from this list, a clinician may use other components of the BASC, such as the PRS and TRS, as part of a functional behavioral assessment paradigm. Given the time-consuming nature of observations, a useful strategy may be to collect teacher ratings from classrooms in which an observation is not practical, and parent ratings to assess differences across settings. Observations are central to the ongoing classroom problem-solving and consultation processes, which are often concerned with the assessment of a child's behavioral adaptation in school, as is discussed next.

Monitoring with the SOS

The SOS is the one component of the BASC Monitor for ADHD that may be applied to all children regardless of their diagnosis or classification. In fact, we know of school districts that use the SOS and Monitor software to evaluate progress toward Individualized Education Program (IEP) objectives, assess effects of prereferral intervention, and assess the effectiveness of various special education programming decisions. Some have used the SOS to assess the impact of social work or special services on classroom behavior. Perhaps more than any other BASC component, the SOS is designed specifically to serve behavioral intervention and evaluation processes in the classroom. We now discuss some possible scenarios and examples of applications of the SOS.

Medical Effects

Marco's parents are resistant to the use of medication with their child. Yet numerous behavioral (e.g., psychotherapy, play therapy, token economy, etc.) and educational interventions (e.g., peer tutor, after-school tutor, summer school, preferential seating, etc.) have failed. The SOS may help such reluctant parents gauge the effects of pharmacological interventions on Marco's classroom behavior in a manner that they perceive as more objective than teacher ratings.

In this example, an independent, perhaps even case-blind observer may take SOS observations to evaluate presomatic therapy whenever dosage or medication is changed, or at two or more points after the initiation of therapy (perhaps in as few as 2–4 weeks after the initiation of methylphenidate, or another medication that reaches therapeutic levels rather quickly). The BASC Monitor Software can then graph Part B (momentary time sampling), results that a practitioner can share with parents, physicians, or other service providers and caregivers. Specific behaviors from Part A can be graphed as well, but we would expect individual behaviors to be less reliable indicators of change overall.

In this scenario, practitioners must be able to link somatic therapy to change. To do so, observers should collect SOS data concurrently with changes in regimens. We think that the 15-minute time sampling is adequate for this purpose, both from our experience and from the finding that interobserver reliability did not differ for 15- or 45-minute observations (Lett & Kamphaus 1997). In addition, children receiving certain medications (e.g., psychostimulants, anxiolytics, antidepressants, antipsychotic medications) require careful monitoring of the effects of these drugs on their classroom behavior.

IEP Objectives

Part A was designed specifically to enhance the development of IEP objectives. Behavior from Part A may then be tracked with the repeated rating of Part A, and change graphed by Monitor software. In fact, some statisticians who have expressed concern about an overreliance on statistical significance testing have noted that graphing is one powerful alternative method for data analysis. We have noted how convincing a graph is to teachers, parents, and others.

We suggest, however, that the clinician observe using Part B prior to completing Parts A and C. We think that the vigilance required to complete the momentary time sampling ensures careful observation that leads to a more accurate rating of ongoing behavior intervention plans.

Finally, because three data points are advised to get a reliable trend line, we recommend as a minimum guideline that observers collect data at the outset of the school year (after the child has had a month to adjust to teachers, peers, etc.), at a midway point when it may be convenient to adjust intervention (certainly March or April of the academic year would be too late), and just prior to the annual evaluation of IEP goals.

Prereferral Intervention

The evaluation of such intervention can occur in the same framework advised for the annual evaluation of IEP objectives, but on a shorter timetable. Again, a minimum of three data points are advised even if the intervention is designed to be brief (e.g., a month or two). Consider the following example:

Shaquille is a victim of physical abuse by his mother, resulting in his being placed under foster care for three months. At the same time, his mother is receiving treatment. He is beginning routine counseling sessions at school for the first time. Shaquille also has a history of distractibility and truancy at school.

An observer could track Shaquille's truancy by event recording during this time period and assess his classroom behavior by the SOS during monthly intervals. SOS results could be of some additive value in assessing the value and the effects of the foster-care placement and counseling on his classroom behavior.

School-Wide Interventions

We recognize the impracticality of using the SOS on a large scale, but we do think that it could be used for sampling purposes. To evaluate the effects of a school's violence prevention program, for example, an observer could sample one or two children in each classroom who are deemed to be at risk for aggression. Good evaluation data are crucial for such programs, as evidence of iatrogenic effects has been noted, particularly in peer group interventions (Dishion, McCord, & Poulin, 1999).

The SOS is designed specifically for classroom-based intervention. Practitioners should not consider SOS results, then, when evaluating home-based intervention, unless home- and school-based interventions are linked. For example, a home-based reinforcement program may be used to improve behavior at school.

The SOS provides for an assessment of the frequency of classroom behavior problems. Consequently, practitioners may use SOS results from Parts A and B to identify behaviors in need of intervention. In particular, any behavior problem that a child exhibits or adaptive skill that a child does not exhibit becomes a potential candidate for intervention. A practitioner can assign priority for intervention to problem behaviors of higher frequency and adaptive skills of lower frequency.

The SOS is unique among Monitor components in that it allows practitioners to prioritize behaviors for classroom-based intervention. The SOS also measures how troublesome a child's behavior problems are via the *disruptive* category of Part A. Often, children display a number of behavior problems, making it difficult to prioritize behaviors for intervention (Schwanz &

Kamphaus, 1997). Practitioners can use the ratings of disruptiveness to identify behaviors that should be targeted first for treatment.

SOS Training and Administration

For the most part, the SOS is easy to administer and score, but a few tricks can help the practitioner become fluent with administration. First, as noted above, we suggest that administration begin with Part B, the momentary time-sampling procedure—if for no other reason, because the momentary time-sampling procedure forces the observer to be vigilant. SOS users find that after completing Part B, they have a rich compendium of information on which to base Part A ratings and Part C qualitative information.

Administer Part B First

When arranging the observation session, several procedures are helpful to remember. First, with the SOS the selection of target behaviors to observe is typically unnecessary because the Part B categories require the observer to observe broadly. A new category of behavior could conceivably be necessary in some cases, and space is available for including such a category. Nevertheless, the selection of target behaviors has been done for the observer.

Second, the observer should focus on other aspects of observation that contribute to minimal disruption and valid data collection. Observers should schedule the observation period at a time of day and in a class in which problems are known to be of teacher or parent concern so that target behaviors can be observed. In addition, the examiner, particularly at the high-school or middle-school level, may want to use the SOS also in a class in which problems are not present.

Given concerns about unfamiliar adults in the classroom, the observer should try to minimize disruption by being familiar to the school, as, for example, an employee of the school, or introducing himself or herself to the teacher ahead of time (perhaps even visiting the classroom briefly a few times) in the presence of the students, so that they do not become alarmed. In addition, the ob-

DON'T FORGET

SOS administration should begin with Part B, the momentary time-sampling procedure.

server should take a few minutes to observe the classroom as a whole prior to beginning the formal timing for Part B. This delay helps the students settle down somewhat; this in turn allows the observer to obtain a more accurate sample of the child's typical classroom behavior.

Third, examiners must develop a timing mechanism that enhances their comfort with the 30-second momentary time sampling and 3-second observation period. Many observers simply check their watches to time the intervals for observation and coding. Others make an audiotape with a tone that marks the beginning and end of each 3-second observation. Still other creative ways of timing the observation periods are probably available. Practicing along with the BASC SOS training videotape is the best means of developing the timing procedure (for availability contact American Guidance Services, the publisher, on the Internet at agsnet.com or bascforum.com, or by telephone at 800-328-2560).

Fourth, observers should be aware that in Part B of the SOS, the page for making check marks to indicate the presence of a behavior contains 30 columns. Half of these columns are white and half are shaded blue. The shading is included to help the observer mark all categories within the same observation period. Both sets of columns are needed to have space for 30 observations.

The instructions in the BASC Manual (Reynolds & Kamphaus, 1998) for the SOS should be read carefully before using any part of the SOS, including Part B. Only the BASC Manual includes all of the operational definitions of the behaviors that are coded for Part B and Part A.

Complete Part A Second

After using Part B, the observer can easily rate individual behaviors for Part A. The same behaviors that were previously coded by category for Part B are now coded individually for Part A.

Often, we are asked if a fixed numerical value is used to discriminate between the rating categories of *sometimes, often,* and *almost always.* Such a value is not available. We do not wish to constrain clinicians with an arbitrary number because we want to give them latitude to consider the importance of local context and culture. Clinicians are allowed and encouraged to use their local knowledge to rate the items. We have found that, for the BASC TRS and PRS, this same lack of a priori constraint still permits satisfactory to high reliability and validity indexes (see Reynolds & Kamphaus, 1998).

Finally, Complete Part C

The final portion of the SOS is qualitative in nature and central to the role of the SOS as a classroom consultation tool. This section cues the observer to note changes in teacher position, along with teacher behavior change techniques, that either presage a child behavior of interest *(antecedents)* or immediately follow a behavior *(consequences)*. This sequential analysis is advised for developing theories about the effects of a teacher on child behavior. The classroom consultant and teacher can work together using such information to change maladaptive sequences of events and increase the frequency of adaptive sequences.

Observers can also record other sequences of behavior in Part C. Peer interactions that seem to affect the target child's behavior, for example, may be recorded in the *other* category. These behavior sequences, too, can become tools for intervention.

A SAMPLE CASE

Eugene Williams is a 6-year-old kindergarten student referred to a school-based prereferral intervention team in response to teacher concerns about inattention and hyperactive behavior in class. As part of the assessment process, a consulting teacher observed him on two occasions in the classroom. The first observation, taken in early May of the school year, served as a baseline that would be used later in assessing the effectiveness of behavioral interventions.

These interventions were effective in the short term, as can be concluded from Figure 6.1. The intervention team, using this knowledge, may decide to replicate the interventions at the beginning of the next academic year and collect a third or fourth SOS observation. In this way, the team members can determine whether the interventions used are effective over the long term and can make intervention and referral decisions accordingly.

Use of the SOS as an ongoing evaluation tool is an ideal application of classroom observations. Such data are valuable for guiding many decisions regarding the delivery of interventions and services for behavior problems in schools.

SELF-REPORT VALIDITY

As is well known, the YSR (Chapter 4) does not correlate well with teacher or parent report forms. This lack of correlation, however, should not be confused with a lack of validity. In fact, quite the opposite is true. The YSR possesses considerable evidence of validity. Research has shown the YSR taken in adolescence, for example, to be a better predictor of symptoms in adulthood than the CBCL (Aronen, Teerikangas, & Kurkela, 1999). In addition, the YSR is highly predictive of *DSM-IV* diagnoses (Morgan & Cauce, 1999).

Based on these findings and on their own research, Sourander, Helstelas, and Helenius (1999) concluded that parents and teachers often did not notice child and adolescent problems, thus causing interrater disagreement. They also suggested from these findings that self-ratings are important to ensure that large numbers of children with problems are not debarred from needed services simply because adults are not aware of all the problems that they face. From this vantage point, direct classroom observation has an indispensable role to play in the assessment of children and adolescents.

A LAST WORD

In two respects, the assessment of children and adolescents is one of the most pivotal occupations in which anyone can engage. The days of youth are a fulcrum in a person's life, a delta from which later characteristics flow: later disorder and adaptiveness, aloneness and relatedness, successes and failures, joys and sorrows. Moreover, an assessment touches and shapes all these critical aspects of a person's development. Viewed in this way, assessment is at the very center of human life, and few if any activities can match its importance and great influence. When we see, therefore, how profoundly assessment can influence even history itself, we know that we have a tool worth honing and using with the greatest possible care.

```
Child:  Williams, Eugene R                        Birth Date: 04/15/1995
School: Sheridan Elementary                       Age:       6
Grade:  K                                         Sex:       M

Parents
-------
Kent Williams, Parent                             Gretchen Williams, Parent
10 Quincy Road
Phone: (212) 919-4060    Fax: (212) 411-3030      Phone:                    Fax:

School Contacts
---------------
Jennifer Grace, Counselor                         Phone: (212) 656-1002    Fax: (212) 656-1003
Sheridan Elementary, 99 Lone Oak Trail, Athens, GA 30601

Physician Information
---------------------


Clinician Information
---------------------
```

The BASC Monitor for ADHD is a system for collecting and analyzing information about the behaviors of children
and adolescents being treated for attention-deficit/hyperactivity disorder. This computer-generated report is a
summary of behavioral and treatment information intended to assist in evaluating behavioral change and the
effectiveness of treatment. Guidance on interpretation is provided in the Monitor Manual.

```
                                   Treatment History
                                   -----------------

Code Date Impl. Medication      Dosage     Time(s)     Other Intervention              Time
---- ---------- ---------------- ---------- --------------- ------------------------------- ----------------
A   05/15/2001                                           Classroom behavioral intervent
```

```
                              Behavior Monitor Ratings
                              ------------------------
                        T Scores (M=50, SD=10), Norm Group: General
```

No data.

```
                      Student Observation System (SOS) Report of Time Sampling - Part B
                               Occurrences during 15-minute Observation Period
                      ---------------------------------------------------

Behavior Category           05/01/01 05/31/01
--------------------------- -------- --------
Response to Teacher/Lesson      4        8
Peer Interaction                0        0
Work on School Subjects         5        7
Transition Movement             1        0
```

Figure 6.1 Printout of BASC SOS results for Eugene Williams.

```
Behavior Category               05/01/01 05/31/01
----------------------------- -------- --------
Inappropriate Movement            12        7
Inattention                        9        5
Inappropriate Vocalization         4        1
Somatization                       0        0
Repetitive Motor Movements         9        6
Aggression                         1        0
Self-Injurious Behavior            0        0
Inappropriate Sexual Behavior      0        0
Bowel/Bladder Problems             0        0
```

```
          Student Observation System (SOS) Report of Time Sampling - Part A
                  Occurrences during 15-minute Observation Period
                  ---------------------------------------------------

Behaviors by Category                         05/01/01 05/31/01
---------------------------------------------- -------- --------

Response to Teacher/Lesson
  Listening to teacher/classmate or following
    directions                                    S        S
  Interacting with teacher in class/group         S        S
  Working with teacher one-on-one                 S        S
  Standing at teacher's desk                      N        N
  Other                                           -        -

Peer Interaction
  Playing/working with other student(s)           N        N
  Talking with other student(s)                   S        S
  Touching another student appropriately          N        N
  Other                                           -        -

Work on School Subjects
  Doing seat work                                 S        F
  Working at blackboard or computer               N        N
  Other                                           -        -

Transition Movement
  Putting on/taking off coat                      N        N
  Moving around room (appropriately)              S        S
  Preparing materials for beginning/end of lesson S        S
  Being out of the room                           N        N
  Other                                           -        -
```

Figure 6.1 (continued).

```
Behaviors by Category                              05/01/01  05/31/01
------------------------------------------------ -------- --------
Inappropriate Movement
  Fidgeting in seat                                  F         S
  Walking around classroom                           F         N
  Playing at blackboard inappropriately              F         N
  Being removed from the classroom                   N         N
  Using work materials inappropriately               F         N
  Passing notes                                      N         N
  Copying answers                                    N         N
  Jumping out of seat                                F         N
  Running around classroom                           S         N
  Sitting/standing beside desk (on floor)            F         S
  Sitting/standing on desk                           S         S
  Clinging to teacher                                N         N
  Other                                              -         -

Inattention
  Staring blankly/daydreaming                        S         S
  Doodling                                           S         S
  Looking around                                     S         S
  Looking at hands                                   N         N
  Fiddling with object(s)/fingers                    F         S
  Other                                              -         -

Inappropriate Vocalization
  Laughing inappropriately                           F         N
  Tattling                                           N         N
  Teasing                                            S         N
  Making disruptive noises                           F         S
  Arguing/talking back to teacher                    S         N
  Arguing with student                               S         N
  Talking out                                        F         N
  Crying                                             N         N
  Other                                              -         -

Somatization
  Sleeping/head down                                 N         N
  Complaining of not feeling well                    N         N
  Other                                              -         -

Repetitive Motor Movements
  Finger/pencil tapping                              F         S
  Foot tapping/swinging                              F         S
  Spinning an object                                 S         N
  Rocking                                            N         N
  Hand flapping/waving                               N         N
  Pacing                                             N         N
  Talking/humming/singing to self                    F         S
  Other self-stimulatory behavior                    -         -
```

Figure 6.1 Printout of BASC SOS results for Eugene Williams (*continued*).

```
Behaviors by Category                              05/01/01 05/31/01
------------------------------------------------ -------- --------
Aggression
  Kicking others                                      N        N
  Hitting others with hand                            N        N
  Throwing object(s) at others                        S        N
  Destroying property                                 N        N
  Pushing others                                      N        N
  Stealing                                            N        N
  Other                                               -        -

Self-Injurious Behavior
  Pulling own hair                                    N        N
  Hitting self                                        N        N
  Head-banging                                        N        N
  Eye-gouging                                         N        N
  Biting self                                         N        N
  Eating or chewing nonfood items (pica)              N        N
  Other self-mutilation                               -        -

Inappropriate Sexual Behavior
  Engaging in sexual or imitative sexual behavior
    with a partner                                    N        N
  Engaging in sexual or imitative sexual behavior
    without a partner                                 N        N
  Touching others inappropriately                     N        N
  Masturbating                                        N        N
  Other                                               -        -

Bowel/Bladder Problems
  Enuresis                                            N        N
  Encopresis                                          N        N
  Other                                               -        -

N = Not observed, S = Sometimes observed, F = Frequently observed.
```

Figure 6.1 (*continued*).

SOS Part B Trend Graph
Occurrences during 15-minute Observation

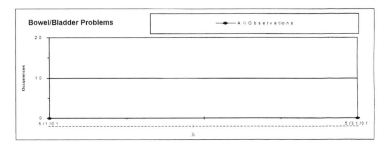

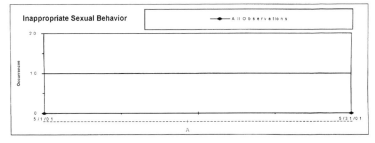

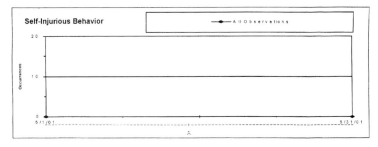

Figure 6.1 Printout of BASC SOS results for Eugene Williams (*continued*).

SOS Part B Trend Graph
Occurrences during 15-minute Observation

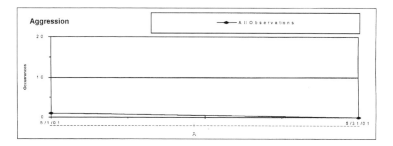

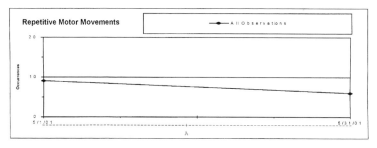

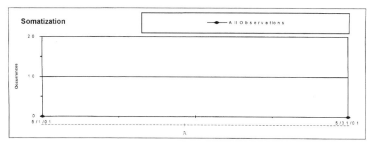

Figure 6.1 (*continued*).

SOS Part B Trend Graph

Occurrences during 15-minute Observation

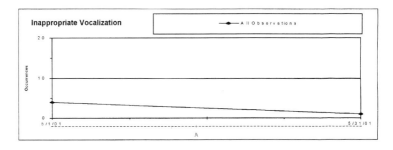

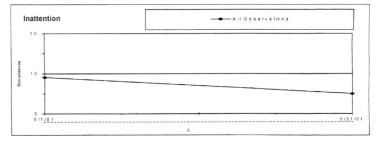

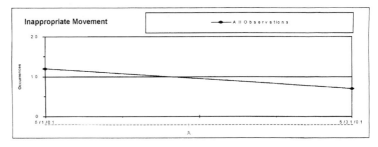

Figure 6.1 Printout of BASC SOS results for Eugene Williams (*continued*).

SOS Part B Trend Graph
Occurrences during 15-minute Observation

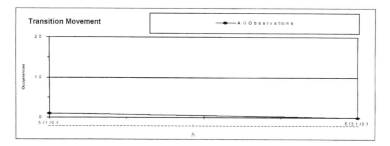

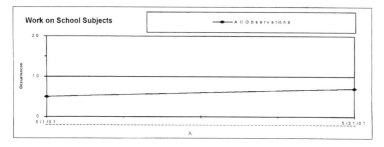

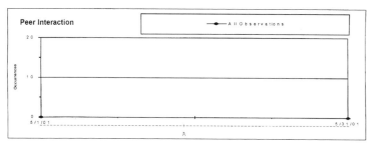

Figure 6.1 (*continued*).

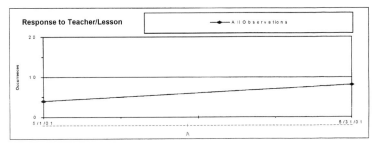

SOS Part B Trend Graph

Occurrences during 15-minute Observation

Figure 6.1   Printout of BASC SOS results for Eugene Williams (*continued*).

SOS Part A Trend Graph
Frequency of Behaviors during 15-minute Observation

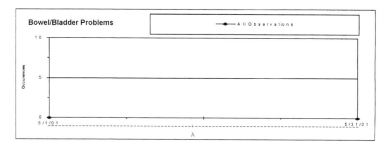

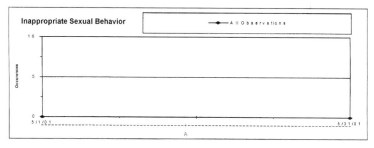

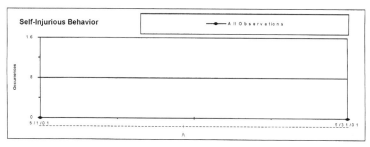

Figure 6.1 (*continued*).

SOS Part A Trend Graph
Frequency of Behaviors during 15-minute Observation

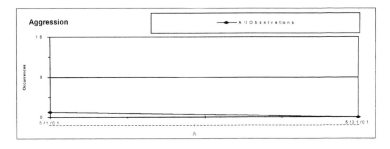

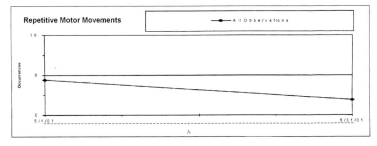

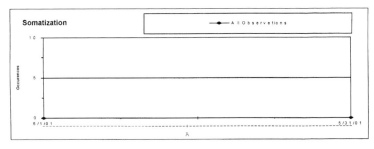

Figure 6.1 Printout of BASC SOS results for Eugene Williams (*continued*).

SOS Part A Trend Graph
Frequency of Behaviors during 15-minute Observation

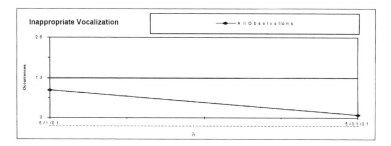

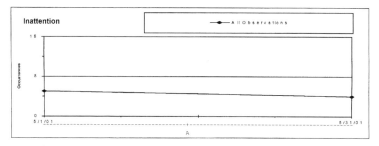

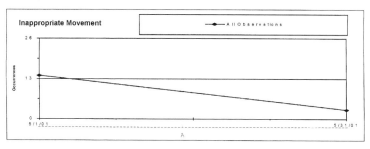

Figure 6.1 (*continued*).

SOS Part A Trend Graph

Frequency of Behaviors during 15-minute Observation

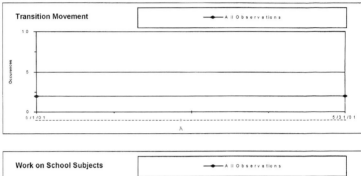

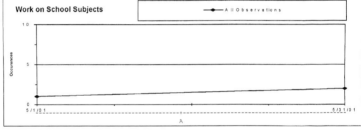

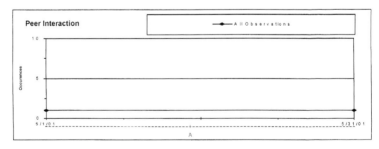

Figure 6.1 Printout of **BASC SOS** results for Eugene Williams (*continued*).

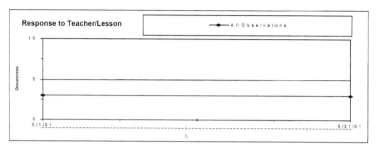

Figure 6.1 (*continued*).

 **TEST YOURSELF**

1. **The limitations of classroom observations include all the following except**

   (a) They cannot provide an in-depth, long-term portrait of a child's behavior.

   (d) The behaviors to observe can be difficult to select.

   (c) Children may not notice an observer in the classroom.

   (b) They can be difficult to schedule.

2. **The primary techniques for observing classroom behavior include**

   (a) event recording, in which a school-based clinician observes and records preselected behaviors.

   (b) time sampling, in which a clinician observes the child at a specified interval, such as every ten seconds.

   (c) setting-derived observation, in which a teacher or related educational professional makes periodic observations.

   (d) Both a and b above.

3. **The Student Observational System (SOS) has which of the following advantages?**

   (a) High interrater reliabilities and recording of adaptive and maladaptive behaviors

   (b) Multiple observation procedures and a generous time-sampling interval

   (c) Operational definitions of behaviors and of time-sampling categories

   (d) All of the above

4. **The SOS assesses the _____ of a child's behavior.**

   (a) frequency, duration, intensity, and antecedent events

   (b) externality, predictability, reactivity, and impact on the classroom

   (c) appropriateness, constructiveness, assertiveness, and degree of control

   (d) enthusiasm, boldness, nonchalance, and directness toward the teacher

5. **In addition, the SOS assesses the _____ of the child's behavior.**

   (a) emotion, thought, and attitude components

   (b) consequences, times, and settings

   (c) biological and social underpinnings

   (d) social and interpersonal impact

6. We suggest that practitioners use the SOS in

(a) evaluating both school-wide and prereferral interventions.

(b) developing IEP objectives and monitoring the effects of medication.

(c) identifying behaviors to target first for treatment.

(d) all of the above activities.

7. When using the SOS, practitioners should

(a) use Part C to assess the child's effect on the teacher.

(b) select each target behavior with great care.

(c) minimize disruption in the classroom.

(d) administer Part A before Part B.

8. Results from Part C can help the classroom consultant and _____ work together.

(a) respondent

(b) practitioner

(c) teacher

(d) parent

9. Part C can also aid in recording

(a) peer interactions.

(b) classroom-level trends.

(c) teacher errors.

(d) parent-teacher interactions.

10. Practitioners can best use Part C to help

(a) develop a profile of the child's interpersonal ability patterns.

(b) encourage the child to exercise creativity and persistence in the classroom.

(c) understand the covert motivations of overt behaviors such as crying and hitting

(d) change maladaptive sequences of behaviors and increase the frequency of adaptive ones.

11. In Chapter 6 we imply that professionals who conduct assessments influence history by

(a) influencing people, who in turn influence history.

(b) gradually changing the nature of assessment.

(c) developing students' capacity for great achievements.

(d) improving the quality of society.

Answers: 1. c; 2. d; 3. d; 4. a; 5. b; 6. d; 7. c; 8. c; 9. a; 10. d; 11. a

References

Achenbach, T. M. (1991a). *Manual for the Child Behavior Checklist/4-18 and 1991 profile.* Burlington, VT: University of Vermont Department of Psychiatry.

Achenbach, T. M. (1991b). *Manual for the Teacher's Report Form and 1991 profile.* Burlington, VT: University of Vermont Department of Psychiatry.

Achenbach, T. M. (1991c). *Manual for the Youth Self-Report and 1991 profile.* Burlington, VT: University of Vermont Department of Psychiatry.

Achenbach, T. M. (1992). *Manual for the Child Behavior Checklist/2-3 and 1992 profile.* Burlington, VT: University of Vermont Department of Psychiatry.

Achenbach, T. M. (1993). *Empirically based taxonomy: How to use syndromes and profile types derived from the CBCL/4-18, TRF, and YSR.* Burlington, VT: University of Vermont Department of Psychiatry.

Achenbach, T. M. (1997a). *Guide for the Caregiver-Teacher Report Form for ages 2–5.* Burlington, VT: University of Vermont Department of Psychiatry.

Achenbach, T. M. (1997b). *Manual for the Young Adult Self-Report and Young Adult Behavior Checklist.* Burlington, VT: University of Vermont Department of Psychiatry.

Achenbach, T. M., & Edelbrock, C. (1983). *Manual for the Child Behavior Checklist and Revised Child Behavior Profile.* Burlington, VT: University of Vermont Department of Psychiatry.

Achenbach, T. M., & McConaughty, S. H. (1987). *Empirically based assessment of child and adolescent psychopathology: Practical applications.* Sage.

American Educational Research Association, American Psychological Association, & National Council on Measurement in Education (1999). *The standards for educational and psychological testing.* Washington, DC: American Psychological Association.

American Psychiatric Association (1994). *Diagnostic and statistical manual of mental disorders* (4th ed.). Washington, DC: Author.

Anastasi, A. (1988). *Psychological testing* (6th ed.). New York: Macmillan.

Aronen, E. T., Teerikangas, O. M., & Kurkela, S. A. (1999). The continuity of psychiatric symptoms from adolescence into young adulthood. *Nordic Journal of Psychiatry, 53,* 333–338.

Asher, S. R., & Wheeler, V. A. (1985). Children's peer status: A comparison of neglected and rejected peer status. *Journal of Consulting and Clinical Psychology, 53,* 500–505.

Beck, A. T. (1967). *Depression: Clinical, experimental, and theoretical aspects.* New York: Hoeber.

Beck, A. T. (1976). *Cognitive therapy and the emotional disorders.* New York: International Universities Press.

Biederman, J., Faraone, S. V., Doyle, A., Lehman, B. K., Kraus, I., Perrin, J., & Tsuang, M. T. (1993). Convergence of the Child Behavior Checklist with structured interview-based psychiatric diagnoses of ADHD children with and without hyperactivity [*sic*]. *Journal of Child Psychology and Psychiatry, 34,* 1241–1251.

Brown, J., & Achenbach, T. M. (1993). *Bibliography of published studies using the Child Behavior*

Checklist and related materials: 1993 edition. Burlington, VT: University of Vermont Department of Psychiatry.

Cohen, J. (1988). *Statistical power analysis for the behavioral sciences.* Hillsdale, NJ: Erlbaum.

Cone, J. D. (1977). The relevance of reliability and validity for behavioral assessment. *Behavior Therapy, 8,* 411–426.

Conners, C. K. (1997). *Conners' Rating Scales–Revised: Technical manual.* North Tonawanda, NY: Multi-Health Systems.

Conners, C. K. (1999). Conners Rating Scales–Revised. In Maruish, M. E. (Ed.), *The use of psychological testing for treatment planning and outcomes assessment* (2nd ed., pp. 467–496). Mahwah, NY: Erlbaum.

Conners, C. K., Sitarenios, G., Parker, J. A., & Epstein, J. N. (1998). The revised Conners' Parent Rating Scale (CPRS-R): Factor structure, reliability, and criterion validity. *Journal of Abnormal Child Psychology, 26,* 257–268.

Coyle, E. L., Willis, D. J., Leber, W. R., & Culbertson, J. L. (1998). Clinical interviewing. In A. Bellack & M. Hersen (Series Eds.) & C. R. Reynolds (Vol. Ed.), *Comprehensive clinical psychology: Vol. 4. Assessment* (pp. 81–96). Oxford, England: Elsevier Science.

Dedrick, R. F., Greenbaum, P. E., Friedman, R. M., Wetherington, C. M., & Knoff, H. M. (1997). Testing the structure of the Child Behavior Checklist/4-18 using confirmatory factor analysis. *Educational and Psychological Measurement, 57,* 306–313.

DeGroot, A., Koot, H. M., & Verhuest, F. C. (1994). Cross-cultural generalizability of the Child Behavior Checklist cross-information syndromes. *Psychological Assessment, 6,* 225–230.

Dishion, T. J., McCord, J., & Poulin, F. (1999). When interventions harm: Peer groups and problem behavior. *American Psychologist, 54,* 755–764.

Doyle, A., Ostrander, R., Skare, S., Crosby, R. D., & August, G. J. (1997). Convergent and criterion-related validity of the Behavior Assessment System for Children–Parent Rating Scale. *Journal of Clinical Child Psychology, 26,* 276–284.

Drotar, D., Stein, R. K., & Perrin, E. C. (1995). Methodological issues in using the Child Behavior Checklist and its related instruments in clinical child psychology research. *Journal of Clinical Child Psychology, 24,* 184–192.

Dunbar, J. R. (1999). *Differential item performance by gender on the externalizing scales of the Behavior Assessment System for Children.* Unpublished doctoral dissertation, Texas A&M University, College Station.

Eiraldi, R. B., Power, T. J., Karustis, J. L., & Goldstein, S. G. (2000). Assessing ADHD and comorbid disorders in children: The Child Behavior Checklist and the Devereux Scales of Mental Disorders. *Journal of Clinical Child Psychology, 29,* 3–16.

Evans, I. M., & Nelson, R. O. (1977). Assessment of child behavior problems. In A. R. Ciminero, K. Calhoun, & H. Adams (Eds.), *Handbook of Behavioral Assessment.* New York: Wiley.

Eysenck, H. J., & Eysenck, M. W. (1985). *Personality and individual differences: A natural science approach.* New York: Plenum.

Flesch, R. (1948). A new readability yardstick. *Journal of Applied Psychology, 32,* 221–233.

Frick, P. J., Kamphaus, R. W., Lahey, B. B., Loeber, R., Christ, M. G., Hart, E. L., & Tannenbaum, L. E. (1991). Academic underachievement and the disruptive behavior disorders. *Journal of Consulting and Clinical Psychology, 59,* 289–294.

Goodman, R., & Scott, S. (1999). Comparing the Strengths and Difficulties Question-naire and the Child Behavior Checklist: Is small beautiful? *Journal of Abnormal Child Psychology, 27,* 17–24.

Groth-Marnat, G. (1990). *Handbook of psychological assessment* (2nd ed.). New York: Wiley.

Hathaway, S. R., & McKinley, J. C. (1942, 1943, 1970). *Minnesota Multiphasic Personality Inventory.* Minneapolis, MN: University of Minnesota Press.

Henker, B., & Whalen, C. K. (1989). Hyperactivity and attention deficits. *American Psychologist, 44,* 216–223.

Heubeck, B. G. (2000). Cross-cultural generalizability of CBCL syndromes across three continents: From the USA and Holland to Australia. *Journal of Abnormal Child Psychology, 28,* 439–450.

Hoy, C., & Gregg, N. (1994). *Assessment: The special educator's role.* Pacific Grove, CA: Brooks/Cole.

Jensen, P. S., Watanabe, H. K., Richters, J. E., Roper, M., Hibbs, E. D., Salzberg, A. D., & Liu, S. (1996). Scales, diagnoses, and child psychopathology. II: Comparing the CBCL and the DISC against external validators. *Journal of Abnormal Clinical Psychology, 24,* 151–168.

Kamphaus, R. W., & Frick, P. J. (1996). *Clinical assessment of child and adolescent personality and behavior.* Boston: Allyn & Bacon.

Kamphaus, R. W., & Frick, P. J. (2002). *Clinical assessment of child and adolescent personality and behavior.* Needham Heights, MA: Allyn & Bacon.

Kamphaus, R. W., & Reynolds, C. R. (1998). *BASC Monitor for ADHD Rating Scales.* Circle Pines, MN: American Guidance Service.

Kaplan, R. M., & Saccuzzo, D. P. (1997). *Psychological testing: Principles, applications, and issues* (4th ed.). Pacific Grove, CA: Brooks/Cole.

Kaufman, A. S., & Lichtenberger, E. O. (2000). *Essentials of WISC-III and WPPSI–R Assessment.* New York: Wiley.

Knight, L. W. (1996). *BASC Parent Rating Scales: Patterns of behavior by gender, race, and socioeconomic status.* Unpublished doctoral dissertation, Texas A&M University, College Station.

Kratochwill, T. R., Sheridan, S., Carlson, J., & Lasecki, K. (1999). Advances in behavioral assessment. In C. R. Reynolds & T. B. Gutkin (Eds.), *The handbook of school psychology* (3rd ed., pp. 350–382). New York: Wiley.

Kreutzer, M. A., Leonard, C., & Flavell, J. H. (1975). An interview study of children's knowledge about memory. *Monographs of the Society for Research in Child Development, 40* (1, Serial No. 159).

Kubiszin, T., & Borich, G. (1996). *Educational testing and measurement: Classroom education and practice* (5th ed.). New York: HarperCollins.

Lett, N. J., & Kamphaus, R. W. (1997). Differential validity of the BASC Student Observation System and the BASC Teacher Rating Scale. *Canadian Journal of School Psychology, 13, 1–14.*

Mayfield, J. W., & Reynolds, C. R. (1998). Are ethnic differences in the diagnosis of childhood psychopathology an artifact of psychometric methods? An experimental evaluation of Harrington's hypothesis using parent reported symptomatology. *Journal of School Psychology, 36,* 313–334.

Morgan, C. J., & Cauce, A. M. (1999). Predicting *DSM-III-R* disorders from the Youth

Self-Report: Analysis of data from a field study. *Journal of the American Academy of Child and Adolescent Psychiatry, 38,* 1237–1245.

Morgan, R. B. (1989). Reliability and validity of a factor analytically derived measure of leadership behavior and characteristics. *Educational and Psychological Measurement, 49,* 911–919.

Nation, P. L. (1996). *The diagnostic efficiency of selected items from the Behavior Assessment System for Children (BASC) Parent Rating Scales and Self-Report of Personality when used with an Attention Deficit Disorder population.* Unpublished doctoral dissertation, Texas A&M University, College Station.

Patterson, G. R., DeBarysche, D. E., & Ramsey, E. (1989). A developmental perspective on antisocial behavior. *American Psychologist, 44,* 329–335.

Ollendick, T. H., & Greene, R. W. (1998). Principles and practices of behavioral assessment with children. In C. R. Reynolds (Ed.), *Assessment, vol. 4* of A. Bellack and M. Hersen, *Comprehensive clinical psychology* (pp. 131–155). Oxford, England: Elsevier Science.

Ostrander, R., Weinfurt, K. P., Yarnold, P. R., & August, G. (1998). Diagnosing attention deficit disorders with the Behavioral Assessment System for Children and the Child Behavior Checklist: Test and construct validity analyses using optimal discriminant classification trees. *Journal of Consulting and Clinical Psychology, 66,* 660–672.

Parker, J. D. A., Sitarenios, G., & Conners, C. K. (1996). Abbreviated Conners' Rating Scales revisited: A confirmatory factor analytic study. *Journal of Attention Disorders, 1,* 55–62.

Ramsay, M. C. (1997). *Causal modeling and regression to the mean.* Paper presented at the annual meeting of the Educational Research Exchange, College Station, TX.

Ramsay, M. C. (2000). *The putative effects of smoking by pregnant women on birth weight, IQ, and developmental disabilities in their infants.* Unpublished doctoral dissertation, Texas A&M University, College Station.

Ramsay, M. C., & Reynolds, C. R. (2000a). Development of a scientific test: A practical guide. In G. Goldstein & M. Hersen (Eds.), *Handbook of psychological assessment* (3rd ed., pp. 21–42). New York: Elsevier.

Ramsay, M. C., & Reynolds, C. R. (2000b). Does smoking by pregnant women influence birth weight, IQ, and developmental disabilities in their infants? A methodological review and multivariate analysis. *Neuropsychological Review, 10,* 1–47.

Reynolds, C. R., & Kamphaus, R. W. (1998). *Behavior Assessment System for Children (BASC) manual.* Circle Pines, MN: American Guidance Services.

Reynolds, C. R., Lowe, P. L., & Saenz, A. L. (1999). The problem of bias in psychological assessment. In C. R. Reynolds & T. B. Gutkin (Eds.), *The handbook of school psychology* (3rd ed., pp. 549–595). New York: Wiley.

Reynolds, C. R., & Ramsay, M. C. (in press). Understanding, identifying, and avoiding bias in ability tests: An empirical review with recommendations. In J. Graham & J. Naglieri (Eds.), *Handbook of psychological assessment.* New York: Wiley.

Reynolds, C. R., & Richmond, B. O. (1985). *Revised Children's Manifest Anxiety Scale (RC-MAS) manual.* Los Angeles: Western Psychological Services.

Sandoval, J., Frisby, C., Geisinger, K., Scheuneman, J., & Grenier, J. (Eds.). (1998). *Test interpretation and diversity.* Washington, DC: American Psychological Association.

Sattler, J. M. (1992). *Assessment of children* (3rd ed.). San Diego, CA: Author.

Schwanz, K. A. & Kamphaus, R. W. (1997). Assessment and diagnosis of ADHD. In W. N. Bender (Ed.), *Understanding ADHD: A practical guide for teachers and parents.* Upper Saddle River, NJ: Merrill-Prentice Hall.

Semrud-Clikeman, M. (1991). ADHD and major depression in children and adolescents. *Child Assessment News, 1,* 1–7.

Shapiro, E. S., & Kratchowill, T. R. (Eds.). (2000). *Behavioral assessment in schools: Theory, research, and clinical foundations.* (2nd ed.). New York: Guilford.

Shaughency, E. A., & Hynd, G. W. (1989). Attentional control systems and the Attention Deficit Disorders (ADD). *Learning and Individual Differences, 1,* 423–449.

Sourander, A., Helstelas, L., & Helenius, H. (1999). Parent-adolescent agreement on emotional and behavioral problems. *Social Psychiatry and Psychiatric Epidemiology, 34,* 657–663.

Steingard, R., Biederman, J., Doyle, A., & Sprich-Buckminster, S. (1992). Psychiatric comorbidity in attention deficit disorder: Impact on the interpretation of Child Behavior Checklist results. *Journal of the American Academy of Child & Adolescent Psychiatry, 31,* 449–454.

Tiffen, K., & Spence, S. H. (1986). Responsiveness of isolated versus rejected children to social skills training. *Journal of Child Psychology and Psychiatry, 27,* 343–355.

Vaughn, M. L., Riccio, C. A., Hynd, G. W., & Hall, J. (1997). Diagnosing ADHD Predominantly Inattentive and Combined subtypes: Discriminant validity of the Behavior Assessment System for Children and the Achenbach Parent and Teacher Rating Scales. *Journal of Clinical Child Psychology, 26,* 249–257.

Volkmar, F. R., Sparrow, S. S., Goudreau, D., Cicchetti, D. V., Paul, R., & Cohen, D. J. (1987). Social deficits in autism: An operational approach using the Vineland Adaptive Behavior Scales. *Journal of the American Academy of Child and Adolescent Psychiatry, 26,* 156–161.

Wainwright, A. (1996). *Conners' Rating Scales: Over 25 years of research.* North Tonawanda, NY: Multi-Health Systems.

Weinstein, C. E., & MacDonald, J. D. (1986). Why does a school psychologist need to know about positive learning strategies? *Journal of School Psychology, 24,* 257–265.

Weiss, G., & Hechtman, L. T. (1993). *Hyperactive children grown up: ADHD in children, adolescents, and adults.* New York: Guilford Press.

Zelko, F. A. (1991). Comparison of parent-completed behavior rating scales: Differentiating boys with ADD from psychiatric and normal controls. *Developmental and Behavioral Pediatrics, 12,* 31–37.

Zukerman, M. (1979). *Sensation seeking: Beyond the optimal level of arousal.* Hillsdale, NJ: Erlbaum.

Annotated Bibliography

Coyle, E. L., Willis, D. J., Leber, W. R., & Culbertson, J. L. (1998). Clinical interviewing. In A. Bellack & M. Hersen (Series Eds.) & C. R. Reynolds (Vol. Ed.), *Comprehensive clinical psychology: Vol. 4. Assessment* (pp. 81–96). Oxford, England: Elsevier Science.

Coyle and his colleagues have provided a detailed review of the purpose and method of the clinical interview, paying special attention to developmental considerations in interviewing. The chapter includes a special section on interviewing children, including preschoolers, and a special section on interviewing parents. Coyle and his colleagues view the clinical interview as an extremely important component of diagnosis and treatment formulation. We agree that interviews are crucial to the overall process and find the approach presented here to be especially useful.

Fletcher-Janzen, E., & Reynolds, C. R. (Eds.) (2002). *Diagnostic reference manual of childhood disorders.* New York: Wiley.

This edited work is a compilation of information that is disorder-specific and formatted consistently across all disorders represented. For approximately 800 disorders, ranging from obscure problems such as Soto's syndrome to more common disorders like Tourette's syndrome, phenylketonuria, and galactosemia, various experts present the natural history and etiology of each disorder, diagnostic keys, basic treatment approaches, expected outcomes, and implications for special education intervention. Physical, cognitive, emotional, and behavioral aspects of each disorder are noted and special attention is given to improving diagnostic accuracy.

Goldstein, S. (1999). Attention-deficit/hyperactivity disorder. In S. Goldstein & C. R. Reynolds (Eds.), *Handbook of neurodevelopmental and genetic disorders in children* (pp. 154–184). New York: Guilford.

In this chapter, Goldstein provides strong conceptual and empirical reviews of the current state of thought on ADHD. Genetic, behavioral, and neuroanatomical views are presented along with the myriad of definitional problems present in the field. Goldstein explains well and critiques the DSM-IV criteria and relates current diagnostic issues well. Practical recommendations for diagnosis and intervention are provided.

Kamphaus, R. W., & Frick, P. J. (2002). *Clinical assessment of child and adolescent personality and behavior* (2nd ed.). Boston: Allyn & Bacon.

The second edition of this successful text provides a scientific context for understanding psychological testing of children and adolescents who are referred for assessment and diagnosis of behavioral and emotional problems. This text covers topics related to this process with strong depth (theories of diag-

nosis) and breadth (disorders such as ADHD and autism). In addition, practical guidelines for using individual tests in clinical practice are provided, including up-to-date information regarding ethical issues and standards of practice. According to Kamphaus and Frick, the most critical component in choosing a method of assessment and interpreting assessment data is an understanding of what one is trying to measure. This volume is an effective tool for understanding the practice of psychological testing. Its writing level is appropriate for practitioners and graduate students in clinical psychology, school psychology, and counseling psychology.

Kamphaus, R. W., Reynolds, C. R., & Imperato-McCammon, C. (1999). Roles of diagnosis and classification in school psychology. In C. R. Reynolds & T. B. Gutkin (Eds.), *The handbook of school psychology* (3rd ed., pp. 292–306). New York: Wiley.

Diagnosis and classification of children into diagnostic groups to receive services is a perpetual controversy in school psychology and related disciplines. This chapter reviews selected issues of diagnosis, including the uses of diagnostic systems, current dominant systems of classification in childhood psychopathology, the classification system of the IDEA, and dimensional systems typically of empirical derivation. The effects commonly attributed to diagnosis are reviewed, as well as some potential problems of the failure to diagnose. The concept of assessment as the ongoing development of an understanding of the individual is contrasted with the simple eligibility decisions prevalent in schools. The link between diagnosis and treatment is emphasized.

Kratochwill, T., Sheridan, S., Carlson, J., & Lasecki, K. L. (1999). Advances in behavioral assessment. In C. R. Reynolds & T. B. Gutkin (Eds.), *The handbook of school psychology* (3rd ed., pp. 350–382). New York: Wiley.

This chapter provides a comprehensive review of behavioral assessment, focusing primarily on its application in the domain of academic and social problems in school psychology. The authors review the common characteristics of various approaches to behavioral assessment and provide a conceptual framework, tracing key historical features from the 1970s to the late 1990s. The rest of the chapter is organized around methods of behavioral assessment, including behavioral interviewing. Self-monitoring is also reviewed in detail and contrasted with other methods of assessment. Detailed guidelines for the selection of target behaviors for intervention strategies are provided.

Maruish, M. E. (Ed.). (1999). *The use of psychological testing for treatment planning and outcomes assessment* (2nd ed.) Mahwah, NJ: Erlbaum.

This work of just over 1,500 pages provides the single most comprehensive source on using psychological tests in intervention planning currently available. Chapters range from global, conceptual reviews (Chapters 1–8) to instrument-specific treatments (Chapters 9–45). Of special interest to our readers, the authors of the BASC, CBCL, and the CRS-R have chapters on the use of these instruments for treatment planning and outcomes assessment. Many other scales of interest to those who use these three instruments are found in this work; the RCMAS, MMPI-A, Children's Depression Inventory, and the Child Health Questionnaire are also addressed.

Pliszka, S. R., & Olvera, R. L. (1999). Anxiety disorders. In S. Goldstein & C. R. Reynolds (Eds.), *Handbook of neurodevelopmental and genetic disorders in children* (pp. 216–246). New York: Guilford.

Anxiety disorders can present with the outward symptoms of many childhood problems. Anxious children may appear inattentive, impulsive, aggressive, or fearful. Pliszka and Olvera note the numerous problems that can be present in such children and note the fundamental disagreements in the field related to basic nomenclature, diagnosis, and treatment of anxiety disorders in children. The role of anxiety in learning and disorders and related conditions is noted throughout the chapter. A review of definitions and prevalence rates reveals anxiety disorders to be relatively common in children and adolescents. Anxiety disorders are comorbid with many other childhood disorders, including ADHD, Conduct Disorder, Oppositional Defiant Disorder, and Major Depressive Disorder, and anxiety is often present as a symptom in the context of numerous other psychiatric disturbances. Pliszka and Olvera cover these issues well. They then review a variety of family and genetic studies of anxiety before moving on to a strong and useful review of the neurobiology of anxiety disorders. Clinical assessment methods, including interviewing and formal testing procedures such as rating scales and psychological tests, are reviewed and recommendations are made for their application. This chapter is useful to anyone who evaluates childhood psychopathology, as well as to those who provide or recommend treatment strategies. The chapter closes with a solid review of treatment approaches and with more detailed coverage of obsessive-compulsive disorder, a disorder of the externalization of anxiety.

Prevatt, F. F. (1999). Personality assessment in the schools. In C. R. Reynolds & T. B. Gutkin (Eds.), *The handbook of school psychology* (3rd ed., pp. 434–451). New York: Wiley.

In this chapter, Prevatt provides a model for effective personality assessment in public school; the model is consistent with special-education law. Multimodal assessment and the integration of both objective and projective techniques are emphasized. Specific methods reviewed include the BASC, the CBCL, interviewing, projective drawings, storytelling techniques, and the Rorschach. Prevatt promotes an outcome-based approach, emphasizing effective interventions that consider the child, the school, the family, and the community.

Riccio, C. A., Reynolds, C. R., & Lowe, P. A. (2001). *Clinical applications of continuous performance tests: Measuring attention and impulsive responding in children and adults.* New York: Wiley.

Continuous performance tests (CPTs) have been proffered as a panacea for diagnosis of ADHD. This book-length treatment of the now-enormous 40-year history of CPT presents a different perspec-

tive on how the tests should be used. Riccio, Reynolds, and Lowe review information from over 400 studies involving CPTs and various diagnostic groups, reporting that CPTs are highly sensitive performance-based measures of attention problems and impulsive responding. This makes the CPT a useful adjunct to impressionistic behavior rating scales. The authors begin with a tutorial on the neurobiology of attention, discussing both neurochemistry and neuropsychological models of executive control. Next, they describe the major paradigms surrounding CPTs suggested for clinical use and the differences between them. The volume presents a review of technical adequacy and standardization of each major paradigm, followed by chapters on the sensitivity and specificity of CPTs in the diagnosis of disorders of childhood and adults. The relationship of CPTs to other tests is also reviewed and the uses of CPTs in diagnosis and in monitoring treatment effects, especially psychopharmacological effects, are noted. This work provides a reference source for everyone who evaluates children with behavioral problems associated with disorders of attention, executive control, or both, in either using CPTs as a component of the diagnostic process or interpreting reports from those who do. As Hynd notes in the foreword, CPTs can vary considerably, and performance can be impaired by a host of disorders, making a comprehensive reference such as this text not simply useful, but necessary.

Sechrest, L., Stickle, T. R., & Stewart, M. (1998). The role of assessment in clinical psychology. In A. Bellack & M. Hersen (Series Eds.) & C. R. Reynolds (Vol. Ed.), *Comprehensive clinical psychology: Vol. 4. Assessment* (pp. 1–32). Oxford, England: Elsevier Science.

In this chapter, Sechrest, Stickle, and Stewart describe and criticize the development and application of clinical assessment in the field of clinical psychology. Their review is at times blistering in its criticisms of subjective methods, especially the Rorschach. Although they view multimodal, objective methods such as behavior rating scales positively, the authors maintain that psychological testing and diagnosis are much more difficult and complicated than generally understood in actual practice. Overall, they view the field's progress over the course of the last century as disappointing; they express particular dismay over the lack of development of more sophisticated theories to guide assessment methods and strategies. This challenging review of assessment practice and methods deserves attention because it comes from Sechrest, a leader in the field of psychological testing and assessment.

Tramontana, M. G., & Hooper, S. R. (1997). Neuropsychology of child psychopathology. In C. R. Reynolds & E. Fletcher-Janzen (Eds.), *The handbook of clinical child neuropsychology* (2nd ed., pp. 120–139). New York: Plenum.

This chapter provides a conceptual schema for understanding the neuropsychological basis of many child and adolescent behavior disorders. The authors review key conceptual issues in the field, including the role and prevalence of brain dysfunction in childhood psychopathology. A summary of findings associated with selected areas of childhood psychopathology (i.e., autism, ADHD, conduct disorder, depression, and anxiety disorders) is presented and the research is critically evaluated. Clinicians should find this work useful in conceptualizing and understanding the nature of many childhood be-

havioral disorders and can find several related chapters in the parent volume as well (especially Chapters 3, 8, and 30).

Wiggins, J., & Trobst, K. K. (1998). Principles of personality assessment. In A. Bellack & M. Hersen (Series Eds.) & C. R. Reynolds (Vol. Ed.), *Comprehensive clinical psychology: Vol. 4. Assessment* (pp. 349–370). Oxford, England: Elsevier Science.

This work presents a broad, systematic, and coherent review of the most fundamental traditions and methods of personality assessment, including their history and current status. Five fundamental paradigms of personality assessment are detailed: psychodynamic, personological, multivariate, empirical, and interpersonal. This work provides a view that contrasts sharply with that of Sechrest and his colleagues, whose work is also annotated in this bibliography. Addressing each of the five major frameworks for personality assessment, Wiggins and Trobst review its history, examine its conceptual framework, provide examples of its instrumentation, explain its interpretive principles, and describe its applications and current status.

INDEX

About the Authors

Michael C. Ramsay earned his doctorate in 2000 from Texas A&M University in College Station, where he obtained Lechner and Regents Fellowships and pursued an advanced research, measurement, and statistics program with a focus on test development in the Department of Educational Psychology. His dissertation is a multivariate analysis of medical research examining the effects of maternal smoking on infant birth weight, developmental disabilities, and intelligence as measured by IQ. An internationally read author, he maintains an ongoing research program developing innovative methodologies and data collection techniques. His research interests include test bias, bilingual assessment, intellectual achievement of ethnic groups, construction and analysis of psychometric tests, multivariate evaluation of medical research, structural equation modeling, and evidence for causation. Dr. Ramsay has consulted with numerous research clients, taught university-level statistics and cognitive psychology courses, presented workshops and lectures on advanced statistical techniques and computer applications, authored and coauthored many scholarly publications, and reviewed for numerous journals and professional associations, including the *Archives of Clinical Neuropsychology* and the American Educational Research Association. In addition, he collaboratively develops and conducts individual training programs with challenged, adult second language learners. Large-scale investigations directed or codirected by Dr. Ramsay at the university have included the first Texas statewide survey of student 504 classification, conducted with the Educational Research and Evaluation Laboratory for the Texas Education Agency, and an extensive series of focus groups and surveys conducted with the Department of Measurement and Research Services for the Department of Residence, Life, and Housing. Additional research has included empirical evaluation of on-site internship programs in school districts with large minority and economically disadvantaged populations; analysis of the efficacy of educational programs for second language learners; and pioneering examination of the English and Spanish Editions of the Metropolitan Readiness Tests, the latter two in a joint appointment with Sam Houston State University.

Cecil R. Reynolds earned his doctorate in 1978 from the University of Georgia under the tutelage of Dr. Alan S. Kaufman. Prior to joining the Texas A&M University faculty in 1981, Dr. Reynolds was a faculty member at the University of Nebraska–Lincoln, where he served as Associate Director and Acting Director of the Buros Institute of Mental Measurement, after writing the grants and proposals to move the Institute to Nebraska following the death of its founder, Oscar Buros. His primary research interests include all aspects of psychological assessment, with particular emphasis on assessment of memory, emotional and affective states and traits, and issues of cultural bias in testing. He is the author of more than 300 scholarly publications and is author or editor of 34 books, including *Clinical Applications of Continuous Performance Tests, Handbook of School Psychology,* the *Encyclopedia of Special Education,* and the *Handbook of Clinical Child Neuropsychology.* He is the author of several widely used tests of personality and behavior, including the Behavior Assessment System for Children (BASC) and the Revised Children's Manifest Anxiety Scale. He is also senior author of the Test of Memory and Learning and the Clinical Assessment Scales for the Elderly. He has a clinical practice in Bastrop, TX, where he treats trauma victims and individuals with traumatic brain injury.

Dr. Reynolds is a diplomate in clinical neuropsychology from the American Board of Professional Neuropsychology, of which he is also a past president, in school psychology from the American Board of Professional Psychology, and he is a diplomate of the American Board of Forensic Examiners. He is a past president of the National Academy of Neuropsychology, APA Divisions 5 (Evaluation, Measurement, and Statistics) and 40 (Clinical Neuropsychology). He is editor in chief of *Archives of Clinical Neuropsychology* and serves on the editorial boards of 11 other journals in the field. Dr. Reynolds has received multiple national awards, including the Lightner Witmer Award and the early career awards from APA Divisions 5 and 15 (Educational Psychology). He is a corecipient of the Robert Chin Award from the Society for the Psychological Study of Social Issues and a MENSA best research article award. In 1999 Dr. Reynolds received the Senior Scientist Award from APA's Division of School Psychology. In 2000 he received the National Academy of Neuropsychology's Distinguished Neuropsychologist Award, the Academy's highest award for research accomplishments. His service to the profession and to society has also been recognized through the President's Gold Medal of the National Academy of Neuropsychology, the Academy's